The Mariner's Trivia Book

RUSTIE BROWN

AUTHOR OF

The Titanic, the Psychic and the Sea

FOREWORD BY

Ronald W. Warwick

Chief Officer of *Queen Elizabeth 2*

Blue Harbor Press

P.O. Box 1028
Lomita, CA 90717

Published by

BLUE HARBOR PRESS ● P.O. Box 1028, Lomita, CA 90717

ISBN 0-9605278-1-8

Library of Congress Card Number: 85-073570

Printed in the United States of America
First Printing: June, 1986
Cover and Symbols Design: Ken Marschall

Dedicated in memory

of

Edwina Troutt MacKenzie

1884 - 1984

My dear friend and *Titanic* survivor.

Acknowledgments

Don Lynch, Barbara Cable, Chief Officer Ronald Warwick, Nancy Brown, Mike Brown, Marcia McGovern, Lila Morgan, Walter Lord, Ann Rumery, Bob Lennon, Marshall Drew, Eva Hart, Ruth Blanchard, Bette Wolfe, Charleen Roberts, Wayne Pierce, Eric and Joseph Sauder, Robert Forrest, Gene and Dottie Parks, Dorothy Hoffman, Bill and Mary Ann MacKenzie, Sally and Cheryl at Mike's Marine Hardware in San Pedro, Jack and Joanne Reilly, Bill and Shirley Grant, Lorraine Finnie, Mackie Haviland, Agnes Zehrung, Hector Felix, Joe and Shirlee Valensi, Bernie Petitjean, Linda Huth, George and Catherine Bolton, Shelley Dziedzic, Jim and Marilyn Manley, Tom Tormey, Wayne Wheeler, Ken Black, Paula Salo, Regis Ginn, Bob Holt, Phyllis Nelson, Bob and Teddi Peters, Tim Yoder, George Bryan, John and Muriel Olguin, Don and Caroline Grounds, Roland and Donna Speakman, Captain Bob Arnott of the *QE2*, Captain Torbjorn Hauge of the *Norway*, Captain Narciso Fossati of the *Carnivale*, Captain Hartvig von Harling of the *Starward*, Palos Verdes Library, Long Beach Library, Los Angeles Library, Torrance Library, Lomita Library, San Pedro Library and all the diligent librarians therein. Special thanks to my husband, Howard Brown, whose supportive help has been anything but trivial.

Foreword

The pursuit of trivia has long been a satisfying quest to its devotees. Recently it has become popular and many more people now enjoy its fascination and the learning pleasure that it gives.

Since the marine area provides a wealth of arcane, interesting and captivating facts, a book such as this has long been overdue. Rustie Brown, with her inquiring nature and long association with things nautical, fulfills that need and provides the marine aficionado with many hours of enjoyable reading and fun.

My own favorite pursuit is to talk to those I meet on shipboard about our language. There are few people that know that many of the words and expressions that are commonly used today were first coined by seafarers of years ago. The origins of some of these, forgotten over the passage of time, will be found herein.

Those who go to sea in ships seem to have a never ending number of questions of endless variety for the mariner. Rustie Brown has certainly eased our task, so please read on!

RONALD W. WARWICK
CHIEF OFFICER
SS *QUEEN ELIZABETH 2*   *At sea 12 May, 1985*

Symbols

Q: Why does the author place a symbol before each
     question?

A: For your convenience and to give you a choice.

Some people are more interested in liners than in literature. Some people are lighthouse lovers and aren't very
enthusiastic about the sex life of seahorses. The use of
symbols gives you, the reader, an opportunity to pick
and choose particular categories of questions if you so
desire. Symbol significance is as follows:

Literature, music, quotations, art and movies.

People (pirates, etc., groups of people).

Geography (harbors, coastlines, beaches, places
and locations).

Naval/Military.

Myths, superstitions and traditions.

Definitions, nautical terms, nicknames, meanings, expressions, abbreviations and maritime law.

Sail.

Oceanographic sciences and marine biology.

Lighthouses.

Liners and powered vessels.

Navigation, navigational instruments, communication and flags.

Miscellaneous/whatever.

These questions may be used in conjunction with other trivia games, given individual points (such as 10 points for a pirate question), for increasing your knowledge or just for the fun of it. Bon Voyage!

1. On what island does Boston Light, one of the oldest lighthouses in the United States, stand?

2. Blackbeard's Tower in the Bahamas is supposedly where pirate Blackbeard looked for prey. What was Blackbeard's real name?

3. What shape is a "burgee" flag (used especially by ships for signals or identification)?

4. In John Masefield's famous poem *what* or *who* gives "A clear call that may not be denied"?

5. What is the difference between "flotsam" and "jetsam"?

1.   LITTLE BREWSTER ISLAND.

2.   EDWARD TEACH.

3.   SWALLOWTAILED.

4.   *THE SEAS* — "I MUST GO DOWN TO THE SEAS AGAIN," FROM "SEA FEVER."

5.   *FLOTSAM* IS FLOATING DEBRIS. *JETSAM* IS GOODS THROWN OVERBOARD TO LIGHTEN SHIP. JETSAM USUALLY SINKS.

6.   What are the first two lines of the original "Anchor's Aweigh"?

7.   What ship rammed the German submarine U-103 in 1918?

8.   What does the "painter" on a dinghy do?

9.   There are three standard colors used for lighted aids to navigation. They are red, green and ______?

10.   What is another name for a map maker?

6.   "STAND NAVY DOWN THE FIELD, SAILS SET TO THE SKY."

7.   H.M.S. *OLYMPIC*.

8.   SECURE IT—A PAINTER IS A LINE AT THE BOW.

9.   WHITE.

10.   CARTOGRAPHER.

11.   In whose honor did the celebrated sailor John Paul Jones change the name of one of his ships to *Bonhomme Richard?*

12.   What does a "Beaufort Scale" tell?

13.   In nautical terms what does the "bitter end" mean?

14.   What was the name of the *ship* in the book *Moby Dick?*

15.   Where, on a boat or ship, would you find a "cringle"?

11. IN HONOR OF BENJAMIN FRANKLIN—AS A COMPLIMENT TO *BENJAMIN FRANKLIN'S ALMANACK* AND THE SAYINGS OF POOR RICHARD.

12. A BEAUFORT SCALE IS A TABLE DESCRIBING 12 STAGES OF WIND VELOCITY.

13. THE LAST PART OF A ROPE, OR THE LAST LINK IN AN ANCHOR CHAIN.

14. THE *PEQUOD.*

15. THE SAIL; A CRINGLE IS A RING SEWN INTO THE SAIL SO THAT A LINE CAN BE PASSED THROUGH IT.

16. "And as the smart ship grew,
In stature, grace and hue,
In shadowy, silent distance
grew the iceberg too,"
wrote what novelist and poet whose initials are
T.H.?

17. What do sailors consider the luckiest thing to be
born with?

18. What is a Blue Nose ship?

19. A part of the ocean near the equator abounding
in calms is called what?

16.   THOMAS HARDY ("THE CONVERGENCE OF THE TWAIN") — VERSE VIII.

17.   A "CAUL" (AMNIOTIC MEMBRANE COVERING HEAD AT BIRTH). BEING BORN WITH A CAUL MEANS YOU CAN NEVER DROWN.

18.   ONE FROM NOVA SCOTIA.

19.   DOLDRUMS.

20.   What were the two main purposes of the pictur-
esque architectural addition of a "Widow's Walk"
on a house?

21.   "I name this ship ________ ________ . May God
bless her and all who sail in her," said Princess
Diana, November 1984. What ship did she name?

22.   What famous playwright, author and poet took
the *Arizona* from Liverpool to New York (in 1882)
and when asked by Customs, "Have you anything
to declare?", answered, "Only my genius."?

23.   What type of ship was the original *Red Jacket,
James Baines* and *Lightning*?

20. OBSERVATION — USED PRIMARILY BY SAILORS, AND YEARS AGO, WHEN A CHIMNEY WAS PLACED IN THE MIDDLE OF THE HOUSE, AN OPENING WITH A RAIL WAS BUILT FOR QUICK ACCESS IN CASE OF FIRE IN THE CHIMNEY.

21. *ROYAL PRINCESS.*

22. OSCAR WILDE.

23. CLIPPER SHIPS.

24. Theodore Dreiser, author of *An American Tragedy,* took the *Kroonland* to New York in April of 1912 instead of taking the *Titanic.* Why?

25. What do the initials L.O.R.A.N. stand for in nautical terminology?

26. What famous ship struck and sank the Nantucket Lightship (#117) on May 15, 1934?

27. What famous liner did Eleanor Roosevelt launch in 1940?

28. In what city is the Peabody Museum located?

24.   IT WAS LESS EXPENSIVE.

25.   LOng RAnge Navigation.

26.   THE R.M.S. *OLYMPIC*.

27.   S.S. *AMERICA*.

28.   SALEM, MASSACHUSETTS.

29. Who invented the screw propeller?

30. Where did a squadron of Navy destroyers pile up on rocks in 1923 with the loss of seven ships and 22 lives?

31. The term "maru" accompanies all Japanese vessels. In Japanese it means steamship, true or false?

32. Albacore fishermen scatter pieces of oily fish to attract albacore and tuna. What are these pieces of fish called?

33. The *Cutty Sark* is preserved in what city in the United Kingdom?

29.   JOHN ERICSON.

30.   NEAR POINT ARGUELLO LIGHTHOUSE, SEVEN MILES NORTH OF POINT CONCEPTION, CALIFORNIA. This was thought to be the most incredible navigational blunder in naval history. An interesting side note to this incident is that in 1984 a scuba diver, Dan Purdie, found the class ring of William Calhoun (great-grandson of John C. Calhoun who served as vice president to President Adams and Jackson) aboard the sunken destroyer *Young* which had been commanded by William Calhoun. Calhoun survived that disaster but died in 1963. His engraved ring was given to his widow (Rosalie) who lives in San Diego.

31.   FALSE — TRANSLATED THE TERM "MARU" CARRIES THE HOPE OR ASSUMPTION OF PERFECTION OR COMPLETE-NESS, BEING DERIVED FROM ITS ORIGINAL MEANING OF A CIRCLE OR SPHERE.

32.   CHUM.

33.   GREENWICH, ENGLAND.

34. In 1833, what President's likeness was the figure-head on the bow of the *Constitution*?

35. What Atlantic liner had a floating stock exchange until the market collapse of 1929?

36. Who wrote *Captains Courageous*?

37. What yacht club in Newport, Rhode Island, is named after a lady lighthouse keeper who saved 18 people from Neptune's grasp?

38. Dana Point, California was named after the author of *Two Years Before the Mast.* Give the full name of this person.

34.   PRESIDENT ANDREW JACKSON.

35.   R.M.S. *BERENGARIA.*

36.   RUDYARD KIPLING.

37.   IDA LEWIS YACHT CLUB IN NEWPORT HARBOR, NEWPORT, RHODE ISLAND.

38.   RICHARD HENRY DANA. Dana wrote the story of the life of a common sailor at sea as it really was at that time. Dana swung over a cliff at Dana Point (on ropes) in order to dislodge some cowhides fellow sailors had tried to throw to the beach below for transporting to their ship.

39.   To the nearest million how much did the City of Long Beach, California pay for the *Queen Mary*?

40.   Near what large city is the Great Lakes "Lighthouse" Marine Museum (also called the Fairport Marine Museum) located?

41.   Has the question of why whales get stranded been resolved and, if so, by whom?

42.   After *what* or *whom* is Pigeon Point lighthouse (between San Francisco and Santa Cruz, California) named?

39. $3.45 MILLION.

40.   CLEVELAND, OHIO.

41.   THE EXACT CAUSE IS NOT KNOWN.

42.   AFTER *CARRIER PIGEON*, A SHIP THAT PILED UP TWENTY
         YEARS BEFORE THE STATION WAS INSTALLED.

43.   Where is the original statue of the "Man of the Wheel" (in memory of fishermen and mariners lost at sea) located?

44.   What does it mean when a ship gives a whistle signal of three short blasts?

45.   What was the name of the Boston-born artist who became famous for his paintings of Maine and the sea?

46.   In what city are the following historic ships on display: *Berkeley* and *Star of India*?

43.   THE "MAN OF THE WHEEL" (ALSO KNOWN AS "THE GLOUCESTER FISHERMAN") IS AT GLOUCESTER, MASSACHUSETTS.

44.   ENGINES IN REVERSE.

45.   WINSLOW HOMER.

46.   SAN DIEGO, CALIFORNIA. THE *STAR OF INDIA* WAS BUILT IN 1863 AND THE *BERKELEY* WAS BUILT AS A FERRYBOAT IN 1898.

47.   What is the name of the instrument used in navigation to ascertain the vertical angle between the horizon and a known heavenly body?

48.   What famous cocktail was named after a United States Line ship of the 1930's?

49.   In the Navy what officer navigates the ship?

50.   What was the *longest* liner ever built?

51.   What is a sailor's nickname for a carpenter?

47.   SEXTANT.

48.   S.S. *MANHATTAN* (1931).

49.   A "NAVIGATING OFFICER" (SPECIALLY APPOINTED), BUT THE CAPTAIN OR COMMANDER IS NEVERTHELESS RESPONSIBLE.

50.   S.S. *FRANCE* (1962), NOW CALLED S.S. *NORWAY*.

51.   CHIPS.

52. In literary maritime history, how did a man named Alexander Selkirk (1676-1721) fit in?

53. What is "Jack Tar" a nickname for?

54. What do sirocco and mistral have in common?

55. In literature, who had himself tied to the mast after blocking the ears of his crew to the sirens' song?

56. Who wrote the screenplay for the movie *Moby Dick*?

52.	HE WAS THE PROTOTYPE FOR *ROBINSON CRUSOE.*

53.	SAILOR.

54.	THEY ARE BOTH WINDS.

55.	ULYSSES.

56.	RAY BRADBURY.

57.   In what time slot does the first "dog watch" on a ship occur?

58.   What was the nickname for "stokers" on a steam-ship?

59.   In New England, what are the young of quahaugs called?

60.   What desert weed has almost identical properties as sperm whale oil?

61.   What was the name of an almost escape-proof harpoon (invented in the mid-1800's) used in the whaling industry?

57.   4 P.M. TO 6 P.M.

58.   BLACK CHOIR OR BLACK GANG.

59.   CHERRYSTONE CLAMS.

60.   JO JOBA (HO-HO-BA).

61.   "TEMPLE'S TOGGLE," INVENTED BY LEWIS TEMPLE AND
        FEATURING HINGED POINTS.

62.   Where does the magnetized needle on a compass (allowing for what is called "variation") always point?

63.   Jane Miletich (at age 22) was the last female stowaway on what great liner?

64.   Who said, "Frankly, I should much rather see the sea's bottom than the moon's behind"?

65.   Fourteen years *before* the *Titanic* sank, a story called "The Wreck of the Titan" appeared in *McClure's* Magazine. Who was the author of the story?

62.   TOWARD THE NORTH POLE.

63.   THE *QUEEN MARY.*

64.   SIR JULIAN HUXLEY.

65.   MORGAN ROBINSON.

66.   In what year was the first S.O.S. sent?

67.   What city is the home of the U.S. Coast Guard Academy?

68.   According to superstition, what is supposed to happen if you whistle aboard a ship?

69.   Sailors from Canada and America ate cranberries, stored in barrels of fresh water to protect themselves from what disease?

70.   What day of the week is considered the *worst* day to launch a ship?

66.   1909. THIS DATE IS ACCORDING TO THE "DAILY PLANET ALMANAC" OF 1979.

67.   NEW LONDON, CONNECTICUT.

68.   YOU WILL BRING ON A STORM.

69.   SCURVY.

70.   FRIDAY.

71. What is the average time it takes for an oyster to produce a pearl?
   1. 1 to 2 years.
   2. 3 to 5 years.
   3. 5 to 10 years.

72. What is the name of a major North American folk art that was very popular with whalers?

73. What is the slang name that pertains to a fruit juice but is used with reference to a British sailor?

74. Which ship has the largest theatre afloat as of this writing?

75. What is the area of a ship's skin between the water line and the rail called?

71.   #2.   3 TO 5 YEARS.

72.   SCRIMSHAW — ENGRAVING ON IVORY.

73.   "LIMEY." LIME JUICE COMBATS SCURVY.

74.   S.S. *NORWAY* (FORMERLY S.S. *FRANCE*).

75.   TOPSIDES.

76. Who is Melville referring to in *Moby Dick* when he says: "For the sea is his; he owns it; as emperors own empires . . . ."?
1. Whales.
2. Nantucketers.
3. Captain Ahab.

77. Norman Island in the British Virgin Islands was supposedly the prototype for what book?

78. Which ocean is the deepest?

79. When the moon is *low* in the sky is there a high or low tide?

76. #2. NANTUCKETERS.

77. *TREASURE ISLAND* BY ROBERT LOUIS STEVENSON.

78. THE PACIFIC.

79. LOW TIDE.

80. On the tall sailing ship *Californian* (a replica of the 1840's Coast Guard Cutter *Lawrence*) a figurehead was unveiled in 1985, modeled after the mythical queen for whom California is named. Who is she?

81. What is another name for a very low tide?

82. Which ocean is the saltiest?

83. "Fight her 'til she sinks and don't give up the ship," said the captain of what ship: *Constitution, Chesapeake* or *United States?*

84. Who wrote: "Home is the sailor, home from the sea, and the hunter home from the hill"?

80.   CALIFIA.

81.   A "NEAP" TIDE.

82.   THE ATLANTIC.

83.   *CHESAPEAKE*, SPOKEN BY CAPTAIN JAMES LAWRENCE.

84.   ROBERT LOUIS STEVENSON, IN A POEM CALLED *"REQUIEM."*

85.   What were Ann Bonny and Mary Read known for in reference to sea-oriented history?

86.   Do the British salute with the palm turned in or out?

87.   Who were the first to use birds in connection with celebrating the launching of a ship?

88.   What poet wrote a group of poems called "Salt-Water Ballads"?

89.   What is the name given to a black flag surmounted by a white skull and crossbones flown by pirates?

85.   BOTH WERE WOMEN PIRATES.

86.   OUT.

87.   THE JAPANESE.

88.   JOHN MASEFIELD.

89.   THE JOLLY ROGER.

90.   In the galaxy of English naval officers, whose name stands out above all? Hint: there is a public square in London named after a battle he won.

91.   In the initiation ceremony of "crossing the line" of the 30th parallel and becoming a "shellback," who is the so-called Ruler?

92.   In the British Navy when an officer is found guilty by court martial, in what *position* is the sword placed on the table?

93.   On the night of April 14, 1912, a young man (with the first name David) was on duty as a night wireless operator in Long Island when he heard of the *Titanic's* sinking and relayed the news to America. This man later became the head of the Radio Corporation of America (RCA). What was his last name?

90.   ADMIRAL HORATIO NELSON (LORD NELSON), WHO WON THE BATTLE OF TRAFALGAR.

91.   NEPTUNUS REX OR NEPTUNE, MYTHOLOGICAL GOD OF THE SEAS.

92.   THE POINT TOWARDS THE ACCUSED.

93.   *SARNOFF.*

94.   What was one reason Alfred G. Vanderbilt drowned in the sinking of the *Lusitania?*

95.   Marie Young, who had been a music instructor to Theodore Roosevelt's children, was a survivor of what shipwreck?

96.   Three metal substances are virtually untouched by the action of sea water over the years. Name two.

97.   Franklin Roosevelt said that he realized every ship had a soul, but his favorite "had one you could talk to." To which liner was he referring?

94.   HE COULDN'T SWIM A STROKE.

95.   *TITANIC.*

96.   PEWTER, LEAD AND GOLD.

97.   *MAURETANIA* (OF 1907).

98. The ancients gave a certain name to the "sacred, ceremonial deck" where they kept doll images of their deities. What deck name still survives this old custom?

99. Linda Morgan, 14-year-old daughter of radio commentator Edward P. Morgan, was catapulted from her bed on one ship to a point 80 feet behind the *Stockholm's* prow and lived to tell about it. On what ship was she originally?

100. What is the name of a powerful, turbulent whirlpool—the most famous being off the coast of Norway?

101. What U.S. city has the Sea Gull Monument (a column supporting a ball, upon which two bronze gulls covered with gold leaf are gently alighting)?

98.   "POOP DECK" — DOLLS WERE CALLED PUPI.

99.   THE *ANDREA DORIA* (INWARD BOUND FOR N.Y. — COL-
       LIDED WITH THE *STOCKHOLM*) ON JULY 25, 1956.

100.   MAELSTROM.

101.   SALT LAKE CITY, UTAH. Reason: in 1848 vast clouds of flying
       insects descended upon the Mormons' first crop and began to
       devour it. The Mormons prayed and a curious phenomenon oc-
       curred — the gulls ate the insects.

102. What important object did Cousteau and Gagnan invent in 1943 for sea-loving buffs?

103. Ship designer William Gibbs requested that his latest design be made entirely of steel and aluminum. Nothing on the ship could be flammable. Yet Gibbs was so superstitious he carried a piece of wood in his jacket for luck. What was the name of the ship?

104. What body of water is located between Alaska and the Soviet Union?

105. What are a "Kona" and a "Williwaw"?

102.   THE "AQUA - LUNG."

103.   THE *UNITED STATES.*

104.   BERING SEA.

105.   EACH IS A TYPE OF WIND: KONA IN HAWAII AND WILLIWAW
        IN THE SOUTH.

106. What famous ship had a fire in a coal bunker on her first trip out to sea?

107. Captain Rostron stated that the "hand of God" was on his ship that zigzagged among the icebergs to rescue *Titanic* survivors. What was his ships name?

108. Where in actuality is Longfellow's "By the shore of Gitche Gumee" in his poem, "The Song of Hiawatha"?

109. What gilded wooden object hangs in Boston's State House?

110. What was the name of William Randolph Hearst's yacht?

106.   THE *TITANIC.*

107.   *CARPATHIA.*

108.   LAKE SUPERIOR.

109.   A CODFISH — AS A MEMORIAL OF THE IMPORTANCE OF
        COD FISHERY TO THE WELFARE OF A NATION.

110.   *ONEIDA.*

111. What famous master-shipbuilder built the clipper ships: *The Flying Cloud, Sovereign of the Seas* and *Great Republic?*

112. What is the name of the waxy solid substance derived from sperm whales and used to make candles?

113. What U.S. lighthouse, built in 1851, was the most expensive (up to that date) at $750,000?

114. What is the most famous "ocean river" or current called?

115. What is the name of the annual list of seagoing vessels (of all nations) telling classifications according to age, tonnage, seaworthiness, etc.?

111.   DONALD MC KAY — THERE IS A GRANITE OBELISK IN HIS
       HONOR AT BOSTON'S CASTLE ISLAND.

112.   SPERMACETI.

113.   ST. GEORGE REEF LIGHT, OFF THE COAST OF CALIFORNIA
       NEAR CRESENT CITY.

114.   THE GULF STREAM.

115.   LLOYD'S REGISTER.

116. What can you expect to happen if you see cat-fish thrashing about in water in an erratic manner?

117. Did the *Titanic* carry 75%, 58% or 84% of her passenger capacity on her maiden voyage?

118. What church steeple in Boston has long served as a landmark for ships approaching the harbor?

119. In the international code of signals what does "C-Charlie" mean?

120. In 1902, what famous author wrote a short story called "Youth"? It was about a fire on board a ship off Java Head. He also wrote *Lord Jim*.

116.   ACCORDING TO RESEARCH TESTS, YOU COULD EXPECT AN EARTHQUAKE WITHIN SIX TO EIGHT HOURS. CATFISH ARE HYPERSENSITIVE TO VIBRATION.

117.   58%.

118.   OLD NORTH CHURCH (A.K.A. CHRIST CHURCH).

119.   YES (AFFIRMATIVE).

120.   JOSEPH CONRAD.

121.   What was the name of Errol Flynn's yacht?

122.   Who wrote "The Rime of the Ancient Mariner"?

123.   What is the name of the lamp that is hand-held and fitted with a finger-operated shutter for sending signals at sea?

124.   Where did the title "America's Cup" for the trophy given in the racing of yachts, originally get its name?

125.   What are hollows between waves called?

121. *SIROCCO.*

122. SAMUEL TAYLOR COLERIDGE.

123. *ALDIS* LAMP.

124. FROM THE SCHOONER *AMERICA* WHICH RACED FOR THE NEW YORK YACHT CLUB AROUND THE ISLE OF WIGHT IN 1851 AND WON. THE PRIZE WAS ORIGINALLY PRESENTED BY THE ROYAL YACHT SQUADRON.

125. TROUGHS.

126. What do the words "Danforth" and "Stockless" refer to in maritime lingo?

127. What was the figurehead of the *Sirius,* the first steamship to cross the Atlantic Ocean to New York?

128. What is the largest seaport in Belgium?

129. Who was the captain of the ship that was, in Greek mythology, supposed to bring back the Golden Fleece?

130. What famous shipowner was made a baronet in 1859 for his contributions to the British shipping industry?

126.   TYPES OF ANCHORS.

127.   THE FIGUREHEAD IS OF A DOG. IT IS NOW IN A MARITIME
        MUSEUM IN KINGSTON-ON-THE-HULL, ENGLAND.

128.   ANTWERP.

129.   JASON.

130.   SAMUEL CUNARD.

131.   What harmless looking animals have done more damage to ships than storms, collisions or bombs?

132.   What ship was built to replace the *Andrea Doria?*

133.   What does LNBs stand for in Coast Guard jargon?

134.   What large city in England (not built directly on a river) has more miles of canals than Venice, Italy?

135.   What was the liner *Vaterland* called the second time around?

131.	SHIPWORMS (TEREDOS).

132.	*LEONARDO DA VINCI.*

133.	LARGE NAVIGATIONAL BUOYS SUCH AS ONE USED ON THE CALIFORNIA COAST OFF DEACTIVATED ST. GEORGE REEF LIGHT NEAR CRESENT CITY.

134.	BIRMINGHAM, ENGLAND (IN THE WEST MIDLANDS).

135.	*LEVIATHAN.*

136. In nautical terminology what is a "Monkey's Fist" and a "Cat's Paw"?

137. Why do the engineers on British ships have dark purple and gold stripes on their uniforms instead of the usual black and gold?

138. In the waters of which country are most sunken treasures found?

139. With what aspect of the Seven Seas is an ichthyologist involved?

140. What alleged pirate said before he was hanged, "I am the innocentest of them all"?

136. TYPES OF SEAMAN'S KNOTS.

137. IN HONOR OF THE ENGINEERS WHO PERISHED ON THE *TITANIC* (KING GEORGE PROCLAIMED THIS MEMORIAL IN 1912).

138. UNITED STATES.

139. AN ICHTHYOLOGIST IS A PERSON WHO STUDIES FISH.

140. CAPTAIN WILLIAM KIDD.

141. As of the late 60's, what was the deepest place in the oceans of the world called?

142. What is another name for the term "ratline" on a sailing ship?

143. It is a sure sign of bad luck to mention the name of a certain animal at sea. What animal?

144. The heads of four _________ _________ were found during the excavation of the Dutch East Ship *Kennemerland,* which sank off the Shetland Islands in 1664 on its way to Indonesia.

145. Sir Walter Scott's poem "Rokeby" is about what mythical ship?

141.   MARIANAS TRENCH (NEAR GUAM).

142.   STEPS OF A ROPE LADDER (ATTACHED TO THE SHROUDS — SMALL TRAVERSE ROPES).

143.   RABBIT.

144.   GOLF CLUBS — ON DISPLAY AT SHETLAND MUSEUM.

145.   THE *FLYING DUTCHMAN*.

146. What or who is a famous occupant of an island (originally called Bedloe's Island) located on the east coast of the United States?

147. Captain William Bligh (of *the Bounty*) returned to the Pacific in 1795 in the ship *Providence* to do what?

148. What term is given to someone who is rendered insensible (by means of drugs or drinks) and finds himself as part of a crew on an outbound ship or in an undesirable position?

149. To whom is the book *Moby Dick* dedicated?

150. What liner flies the United Nations flag by special permission of the U.S. Secretary General?

146.   THE STATUE OF LIBERTY — IN 1956 THE NAME WAS CHANGED TO LIBERTY ISLAND.

147.   CARRY OUT THE ORIGINAL BREAD FRUIT PROJECT (TO PROVIDE INEXPENSIVE FOOD FOR SLAVES WORKING ON SUGAR PLANTATIONS).

148.   SHANGHAIED.

149.   NATHANIEL HAWTHORNE.

150.   S.S. *NORWAY* — BETWEEN 25 & 30 NATIONS ARE REPRESENTED IN THE CREW OF THE SHIP.

151. Why are white oak and teak so popular with builders of yachts?

152. If a person in the British Isles mentions a "coracle," what is being referred to?

153. According to legend and folklore, why is it bad luck to kill a seal?

154. What type of ship is *Sceptre of Great Britain* and *Columbia of America*?

155. What famous English astronomer was to command the *Paramour Pink* (1698) for the *first* sea expedition undertaken for purely scientific purposes?

151.   THEY DO NOT DECAY IN SALT WATER.

152.   A SMALL BOAT MADE BY COVERING A WICKER FRAME WITH HIDE, LEATHER OR A TARP.

153.   BECAUSE SEALS WERE ONCE MEN (OR WOMEN) UNTIL THEY WERE PUT UNDER A SPELL AND FORCED TO LIVE IN THE SEA.

154.   RACING YACHTS.

155.   EDMUND HALLEY (WHO HAS A COMET NAMED AFTER HIM).

156. What is the Mississippi riverboat call for checking two fathoms in depth?

157. In nautical astronomy, what is the term used to denote the point in the heavens directly above the observer?

158. In Admiral Nelson's time, why were buttons put on midshipmen's uniforms crosswise (all the way around the sleeve) instead of up and down?

159. What is the name of the small instrument mounted in front of the compass on a ship indicating how a ship is listing?

156.   MARK TWAIN.

157.   ZENITH.

158.   SO THAT THE MIDSHIPMEN WOULDN'T BE INCLINED TO WIPE THEIR NOSES ON THEIR SLEEVES. AT THAT TIME THE UNIFORMS WERE POCKETLESS.

159.   A COMMUTATOR.

160. Dr. S.M. Kwak is noted in maritime history as:
    1. An advisor on the de-oiling of seabirds.
    2. The first man to come up with the idea of double-hulled ships.
    3. A doctor on board the first ship to be specifically fitted out as a hospital ship in 1860.
    4. None of the above.

161. In real life, what Nantucket whaling ship went down in an incident similar to the fictional *Moby Dick*, in 1820 when attacked by a huge sperm whale?

162. What needless, perhaps deliberate, maritime tragedy occurred on January 9, 1972?

163. There is a legend concerning the "Lorelei" who threw herself into a river in despair over a faithless lover and became a siren who lured fishermen to destruction. Today Lorelei is the name of a rock in what river, in what country?

160.   #1. DR. S.M. KWAK WAS THE LEADING DUTCH ORNI-
THOLOGIST WHO CAME TO CORNWALL, ENGLAND, IN 1967
WHEN THE OIL TANKER *TORREY CANYON* SPILLED
THOUSANDS OF TONS OF OIL NEAR LAND'S END.

161.   THE *ESSEX*.

162.   THE FORMER *QUEEN ELIZABETH*, RENAMED *SEAWISE UNI-
VERSITY*, WAS COMPLETELY GUTTED BY FIRE IN HONG
KONG HARBOR.

163.   THE RHINE RIVER IN GERMANY.

164. What article of clothing is referred to as a "boater"?

165. Sam Lord, whose home base was Barbados in the Caribbean, was a "wrecker." What does the term "wrecker" mean?

166. Which state in the United States has the most lighthouses?

167. How many miles wide is the entrance to New York harbor via Sandy Hook, New Jersey to Rockaway Point, New York—five, seven or ten miles?

168. What was the name of Long John Silver's parrot in *Treasure Island?*

164.   A STIFF BRIMMED STRAW HAT.

165.   ONE WHO CAUSES A SHIP TO WRECK BY HANGING LIGHTS IN THE TREES ALONG THE CLIFFS AT NIGHT, OR BY TYING A LIGHT ON A DONKEY'S TAIL, CAUSING CONFUSION TO APPROACHING SHIPS AND PRECIPITATING DISASTER. WHEN SHIPS RAN AGROUND, PIRATES SUCH AS SAM LORD WOULD THEN PLUNDER.

166.   MAINE. THE REASON IS PROBABLY BECAUSE MAINE'S COASTLINE HAS SO MANY INDENTATIONS.

167.   SEVEN MILES FROM SANDY HOOK TO ROCKAWAY POINT.

168.   CAPTAIN FLINT.

169. How many men were killed in the famous naval battle between the *Monitor* and the *Merrimac?*

170. What do the terms Bell, Can and Nun have in common?

171. What was the duration of the most desperate sea battle in the War of 1812, when Captain Lawrence said, "Don't give up the ship"?

172. What are the holes called that are cut in the bulwarks of a ship to allow water on deck to drain?

173. What famous female singer came to America in 1850 aboard the *Atlantic?*

169.   NONE. AFTER LIEUTENANT WORDEN HAD BEEN BLINDED BY A SHOT, THE *MONITOR* WITHDREW AND THE *MERRIMAC* RETURNED TO NORFOLK.

170.   THEY ARE ALL TYPES OF BUOYS.

171.   15 MINUTES ON JUNE 1, 1813.

172.   SCUPPERS.

173.   JENNY LIND, CALLED THE SWEDISH NIGHTINGALE. WHEN P.T. BARNUM WENT TO GREET HER IN HER CABIN HE FOUND SHIPOWNER E.K. COLLINS ALREADY THERE.

174. In the year 1933, what magazine was most popular with seamen?

175. What gives the Red Sea its peculiar color?

176. What is the largest island in the world?

177. What poetic character said, "Water, water everywhere, nor any drop to drink"?

178. To what or to whom is the statue of "The Little Mermaid" (that is situated in Copenhagen harbor) a memorial?

174.   NATIONAL GEOGRAPHIC.

175.   A BLUE-GREEN ALGAE (WHICH IS FREE FLOATING AND OCCASIONALLY GIVES THE SEA A RED HUE).

176.   GREENLAND.

177.   THE ANCIENT MARINER IN "THE RIME OF THE ANCIENT MARINER."

178.   HANS CHRISTIAN ANDERSEN'S FAIRY TALE OF THE SAME NAME.

179. Do whales and porpoises have a sense of smell?

180. What was the name of the largest U.S. Lightship ever built?

181. What sea creature has eyes that most nearly resemble human eyes?

182. The Virgin Islands are approximately how many miles east of Puerto Rico?
1. 70.
2. 200.
3. 300.

183. How many survivors were there when the cruiser *Hampshire* (on which Lord Kitchener lost his life) was sunk by a German mine in 1916?

179.   NO.

180.   LIGHTSHIP *NANTUCKET* WHICH GUIDED SHIPS FROM
        THE AMBROSE CHANNEL TO THE PORT OF NEW YORK.

181.   OCTOPUS.

182.   #1.   70.

183.   TWELVE SAILORS SURVIVED ON A RAFT.

184. Who is the patron saint of sailors (*not* fishermen, but sailors)? Hint: It's a female saint.

185. Who was the skipper of the yacht *Australia II* that won the America's Cup in 1983?

186. What is the origin of the custom of adorning the bow of a sailing ship with a figurehead of a bare-breasted woman?

187. In a Kenneth Grahame classic, the Sea Rat says, "Take the Adventure, heed the call, now ere the irrevocable moment passes . . ." as he tries to persuade the Water Rat to join him in a sea escapade aboard a ship. From what book is this quotation?

184.   ST. URSULA.

185.   JOHN BERTRAND.

186.   FROM THE SUPERSTITION THAT A STORM WOULD SUB-
SIDE IF A NAKED WOMAN APPEARED BEFORE IT. SHIP-
OWNERS WHO WERE NOT VERY DARING MERELY HAD A
FIGUREHEAD WITH A LOW-NECKED DRESS OR A SHORT
SKIRT.

187.   *THE WIND IN THE WILLOWS.*

188. What color is the "absent flag" indicating that the owner of the boat or yacht is not on board?

189. What is a binnacle?

190. N.A.Y.R.U. is an abbreviation for what organization that has to do with sailing?

191. What lighthouse in New England lost its first two keepers in drowning accidents?

192. What towers 400 feet above the Connecticut River and is the tallest wooden structure on that river?

188. BLUE (RECTANGULAR).

189. A STAND OR CASE FOR A MARINE COMPASS.

190. NORTH AMERICAN YACHT RACING UNION.

191. BOSTON LIGHT. BENJAMIN FRANKLIN WROTE A BALLAD ABOUT THE FIRST INCIDENT BUT, UNFORTUNATELY, THERE IS NO KNOWN COPY NOW IN EXISTENCE.

192. THE GOODSPEED OPERA HOUSE (RESTORED IN 1963) BUILT IN 1877 BY WILLIAM GOODSPEED OF EAST HADDAM, CONNECTICUT.

193. The Cunard Line once had a special flag made for a Mrs. Hargreaves who was the original Alice of *Alice in Wonderland*. What was on the flag?

194. Who is the patron saint of fishermen?

195. Is a shark or a barracuda more likely to attack a man?

196. In the 18th Century why did many sailors have tattoos on their backs?

197. From what poem concerning the sea is: "He prayeth best who loveth best, all things both great and small"?

193.   A SMILING CAT. WHEN MRS. HARGREAVES WAS IN THE UNITED STATES SHE SAID HER FAVORITE CHARACTER WAS THE "CHESHIRE CAT." ON SAILING TO ENGLAND, CUNARD HAD THE SMILING CAT EMBOSSED ON A BACKGROUND OF WHITE.

194.   ST. PETER.

195.   BARRACUDA.

196.   THEY WERE ADVISED BY OLD SALTS TO: "GET A CRUCIFIX TATTOOED TO YOUR BACK AND ANYONE WOULD HESITATE TO WHIP OR LASH A CHRISTIAN SYMBOL."

197.   "RIME OF THE ANCIENT MARINER."

198. What made the *Eleanor, Dartmouth* and *Beaver* famous in 1776?

199. What British Windward Island in the Caribbean made worldwide headlines within the last ten years (prior to publication of this book)?

200. In the famous steamboat race between the *Robert E. Lee* and another vessel, what was the competing ship's name?

201. What color stripes did the *original* Eddystone Light have?

202. From what language is the word "Aye" (as in "Aye, aye, Sir") derived?

198.   THEY WERE THE SHIPS CONNECTED WITH THE "BOSTON
        TEA PARTY."

199.   GRENADA. IT WAS INVADED BY THE UNITED STATES IN
        OCTOBER OF 1983.

200.   THE *NATCHEZ.*

201.   RED AND WHITE.

202.   *OLD* ENGLISH = "YES."

203. Sailors call certain sea birds "Mother Carey's Chickens." What is the common name of this bird?

204. What do the following places have in common: Whitehall, The Breakers, and Vizcaya?

205. Who is Christy Steinman in relationship to the America's Cup races?

206. From what port does the international race with the largest number of contestants in the world depart?

207. Did the distress call "Mayday" derive from English, French, Spanish or German?

203.   PETRELS — PERHAPS NAMED AFTER ST. PETER DUE TO THEIR POWER OF SEEMINGLY "WALKING ON WATER."

204.   THEY ARE ALL MANSIONS BUILT NEAR THE SEA OR OTHER BODIES OF WATER BY MILLIONAIRES. WHITEHALL WAS BUILT BY FLAGLER, THE BREAKERS BY VANDERBILT AND VIZCAYA (IN FLORIDA) BY DEERING.

205.   THE FIRST WOMAN CREWMEMBER OF AN AMERICA'S CUP RACE. SHE WAS NAVIGATOR ON *FREEDOM* IN 1983.

206.   NEWPORT BEACH, CALIFORNIA — GOES TO ENSENADA, MEXICO.

207.   MAYDAY IS DERIVED FROM THE FRENCH *M'AIDEZ* MEANING, "HELP ME."

208. Ulysses carried the symbol of what creature on his shield and engraved on his signet ring?

209. A ship that sank in 1628 was brought up from the deep on April 24, 1961, in Stockholm, Sweden, due to the efforts of a man named Anders Frazen. What was the ship's name?

210. Mrs. Marjorie Merriweather Post was the owner of one of the largest private sailing yachts ever built. What is the name of the vessel she owned?

211. Who discovered the Sargasso Sea?

212. What is a more common name of the fish called hippocampus?

208.   THE DOLPHIN.

209.   THE *VASA*. After 333 years on the ocean floor, the wooden ship, *Vasa*, was raised and thousands of articles discovered on board including guns that (when restored) could still be fired. The *Vasa* sank in water that was deep and cold enough to discourage deterioration.

210.   *SEA CLOUD* (STILL AFLOAT FOR COMMERCIAL LEISURE CRUISING).

211.   CHRISTOPHER COLUMBUS.

212.   SEA-HORSE.

213. What broadcasting executive and baseball team owner was also named "Yachtsman of the Year" four times by the New York Yacht Club? Hint: He also skippered the yacht *Courageous* in America's Cup Race in 1977.

214. In the technology of lighthouses, what does the term "isophase" mean with reference to signaling?

215. What was the name of President Truman's yacht?

216. What is a "Nantucket Sleigh Ride"?
      1. The most dangerous part of whaling.
      2. An exciting feature in the Nantucket winter carnival held on frozen ponds.
      3. A ride on a famous carousel in Nantucket.

213.   TED TURNER.

214.   THE TERM "ISOPHASE" MEANS THAT THE SIGNALS OF LIGHT AND DARK PERIODS ARE OF EQUAL DURATION.

215.   *WILLIAMSBURG.*

216.   #1.   WHEN THE MATE, WITH A BOAT FAST TO A WHALE, GOES IN FOR THE KILL.

217. In mythology, who was the Greek godess of beauty and sexual love who sprang from the foam of the sea?

218. Minot's Ledge light is sometimes referred to as Lover's Light because its flashing signal, 1-4-3, spells out I Love You. Off what state's coast is Minot's Light located?

219. Which of the Great Lakes has the highest waves?

220. What was the name of the dolphin that carried messages and packages for the Navy in the trial run of underwater living in Sealab II?

221. What is a delphinologist?

217.   APHRODITE.

218.   THE STATE OF MASSACHUSETTS, OFF THE COHASSET, MASSACHUSETT'S SHORE (18 MILES SOUTH OF BOSTON).

219.   LAKE SUPERIOR.

220.   TUFFY.

221.   ONE WHO STUDIES DOLPHINS.

222. Failure to display the proper running lights on a boat can bring a penalty of $500 or more. Under whose jurisdiction does this violation fall?

223. In 1944 a commemorative stamp was issued to honor the first steamship to cross the Atlantic from the United States to England. What ship was pictured on this stamp?

224. On what river is West Point located?

225. What famous naval hero said "Damn the torpedoes! Go ahead!" after his best ship was blown up?

226. The white canvas hat that sailors are issued can be used for purposes other than covering the head. Name at least one.

222.   U.S. COAST GUARD.

223.   THE SAVANNAH. THE SHIP LEFT SAVANNAH, GEORGIA MAY 22, 1819 and ARRIVED IN LIVERPOOL, ENGLAND TWENTY-NINE DAYS LATER.

224.   THE HUDSON.

225.   DAVID FARRAGUT.

226.   THE BRIM CAN BE FLIPPED DOWN AND THE CAP USED TO CARRY DRINKING WATER OR FOR BAILING WATER OUT OF A BOAT. THE DESIGN LENDS ITSELF TO EASY FOLDING AND CAN BE CARRIED ROLLED UP IN A SEA BAG.

227. What was the original purpose of the Coast Guard when organized in 1790 under the name the Revenue-Marine?

228. What famous ship, formerly under the command of Lord Nelson, is now on display in Plymouth, England?

229. What ship fired a few salvos and sank the British battlecruiser *Hood*?

230. What was the name of the movie, based upon the life of the boy (Robin Lee Graham) who sailed around the world alone?

231. In nautical terms what is a "rooster tail"?

227.　　TO PREVENT SMUGGLING.

228.　　*VICTORY.*

229.　　*BISMARCK.*

230.　　*THE DOVE.*

231.　　THE ARCHING PLUME OF WATER THROWN UP BY A POWER BOAT'S PROPELLER.

232. What do the letters LST stand for regarding a Navy vessel?

*

233. If you were forced to "abandon ship," and had adequate time to escape, would it be better to slide down a hose or rope, or go hand-over-hand?

234. Godrevy Light in St. Ives, Cornwall, England, was the model for the lighthouse in a novel called *To the Lighthouse*. What famous writer wrote this novel?

235. What Commodore of the Cunard Line had the following honors: American Medal of Honor and medals of the New York Shipwreck Society, and was, for a time, R.N.R. Aide-de-camp to the King of England?

232.   **L**ANDING **S**HIP **T**ANK. The bow section above water on this ship is formed of two doors which can be swung back to allow an unloading (or loading) ramp on a beach. An LST may carry tanks, artillery or people.

233.   GO HAND-OVER-HAND. IF YOU DIDN'T HAVE ON HEAVY GLOVES YOU MIGHT LOSE CONTROL, AS YOUR HANDS COULD EASILY BECOME SEARED AND DAMAGED.

234.   VIRGINIA WOOLF. GODREVY LIGHT WAS REMEMBERED FROM CHILDHOOD HOLIDAYS IN ST. IVES BUT TRANS-PORTED IN THE BOOK TO THE HEBRIDES.

235.   COMMODORE SIR ARTHUR ROSTRON (ONE TIME CAPTAIN OF THE *CARPATHIA* WHO RESCUED *TITANIC* SURVIVORS).

236. What is a "conning tower" on a submarine?

237. It was discovered that a member of the crew of the White Star liner *Laurentic* fell overboard in the mid-Atlantic. How long after the cry of "man overboard" did it take the 19,000 ton liner to stop, turn around and rescue the man?
1. 35 minutes.
2. 45 minutes.
3. one hour.

238. Where did the term "horny" (having a sexual connotation) originate in maritime history?

239. What lighthouse is famous for its two-tone "Beee-Ohhh" fog signal that was recorded for a commercial for deodorant soap?

236. A RAISED STRUCTURE USED AS AN OBSERVATION POST AND OFTEN AS AN ENTRANCE TO THE VESSEL.

237. #1. 35 MINUTES.

238. IN THE EARLY DAYS OF SAILING IT TOOK SO LONG FOR SHIPS TO GET AROUND CAPE HORN — THE NEXT STOP BEING TROPICAL ISLES WITH PRETTY FEMALES — THAT THE SAILORS WERE SAID TO BE "HORNY" BY THE TIME THEIR JOURNEY WAS NEARLY FINISHED. THIS INFORMATION WAS TOLD TO ME IN ALL SERIOUSNESS BY A MUSEUM CURATOR.

239. POINT BONITA NEAR SAN FRANCISCO.

240. Where is the restored World War II submarine USS *Croaker* now docked for public viewing?

241. Whose motto is: "Our Best Today . . . For a Better Tomorrow"?

242. President Franklin Roosevelt's "floating White House" (originally designed as the Coast Guard cutter *Electra*) had a facelift in 1985. What is the name of the ship, as of this writing, that is used as a floating classroom, convention meeting place and museum?

243. In Greek mythology who was Neptune's (Poseidon's) brother?

240.   IN GROTON, CONNECTICUT, ON THE THAMES RIVER NEXT TO GENERAL DYNAMICS WHERE SHE WAS BUILT.

241.   THE SEA SCOUTS, EXPLORER DIVISION OF THE BOY SCOUTS.

242.   THE *POTOMAC*.

243.   ZEUS (JUPITER).

244. What ship had more than twenty tons of paint removed to make it float a quarter of an inch higher in the water?

245. What is Mole describing in *The Wind in the Willows* when he says, "...this sleek, sinuous, full-bodied animal, chasing and chuckling, ..."?

246. Name a popular "packet" square-rigger ship company that contains a color in its title.

247. Tell which of the following areas has the highest frequency of poor visabilities:
1. Georges Banks.
2. Grand Banks.
3. The coast of California.

244. THE *QUEEN MARY*. THE PAINT CHIPS WERE SOLD TO *QUEEN MARY* BUFFS.

245. A RIVER. THE REST OF THE QUOTATION IS "...GRIPPING THINGS WITH A GURGLE AND LEAVING THEM WITH A LAUGH."

246. BLACK BALL LINE OR RED STAR LINE.

247. #2.   GRAND BANKS.

248. What is a Lyle Gun?

249. What famous author didn't agree that "getting there was half the fun" and, after crossing the ocean on *Britannia* in 1842, remarked about the bunks in his cabin "Nothing smaller for sleeping was ever made except coffins"?

250. What is the ladder or walkway called by which one goes aboard a ship?

251. If you saw a movie called *The Last Voyage*, you saw the *actual* sinking of a very famous ship that had been purchased specifically for this purpose. What was the original name of the ship used?

248.   A GUN USED IN LIFESAVING TO THROW A LIFELINE TO A SHIP IN DISTRESS.

249.   CHARLES DICKENS.

250.   GANGWAY, NOT GANGPLANK.

251.   THE *ILE DE FRANCE.*

252. What does it mean when they say in the Navy: "The Smoking Lamp is Out"?

253. What does the term polynya have to do with the sea?

254. Who said, "If you have to ask what it costs to run a yacht, you can't afford one"?

255. What is the second half of the old saying "Red sky at night, sailor's delight"?

256. Into how many points is a modern compass divided?

252.   POSITIVELY NO SMOKING.

253.   A POLYNYA IS AN AREA OF *OPEN* WATER IN SEA ICE —
        SUCH AS IN THE ARCTIC.

254.   J.P. MORGAN.

255.   "RED SKY IN THE MORNING, SAILORS TAKE WARNING."

256.   32.

257. According to Islamic legend, what privilege was the whale entitled to because Jonah spent three days and nights in its belly?

258. When someone in the Navy says, "The sun is over the yardarm," what does that indicate?

259. What is a "fata morgana"?

260. What did the clipper ship *Sea Witch* do that was memorable?

257.   IT WAS AMONG ONLY TEN ANIMALS ALLOWED INTO
       PARADISE.

258.   IT'S TIME FOR A DRINK; FROM THE OLD BRITISH CUSTOM
       OF GIVING THE SAILORS A DRINK OF RUM WHEN THE SUN
       WAS HIGH ENOUGH TO BE OVER THE YARDARM.

259.   A MIRAGE, ESPECIALLY AS OBSERVED ON THE COAST OF
       SICILY, POETICALLY ATTRIBUTED TO THE FAIRY FATA
       MORGANA.

260.   SHE SET A RECORD OF 74 DAYS, 14 HOURS FROM HONG
       KONG TO NEW YORK IN 1849, A RECORD THAT HAS NEVER
       BEEN EQUALED BY ANY VESSEL UNDER SAIL ALONE. HER
       CAPTAIN, ROBERT "BULLY" WATERMAN, HAS BEEN CALLED
       A HERO BY SOME AND A MONSTER BY OTHERS.

261. A person who has been knocked overboard from a small boat should reenter by being hauled over which part of the boat?:
1. The midship section.
2. The bow.
3. The stern.

262. What difficulty did Lord Nelson never overcome during his life at sea?

263. Do etymologists think the expression "son of a gun" originated in the Army or in the Navy?

264. What is the nautical term used to describe the following: the leading edge of a sail; the fluttering of a sail when the boat is pointed too close to the wind or the sail is let out too far?

261.   #3.   THE STERN, ANY ATTEMPT TO GET ABOARD AMID-
SHIPS OR OVER THE BOW CAN END IN A CAPSIZE.

262.   SEASICKNESS.

263.   NAVY. In the days of wooden ships, when sailors were kept in
port (lest they desert), they were allowed "wives" to visit in hammocks slung between guns in the jam-packed spaces between
decks. Sometimes offspring resulted from these encounters —
hence, "son of a gun."

264.   LUFF.

265. Who immortalized the *Constitution,* also known as "Old Ironsides," in a poem of the latter name?

266. What ultimately happened to the beautiful yacht *America,* after which the America's Cup Race was named?

267. Where is a wooden float called a "camel" placed on a boat?

268. On which sleeve do ordinary United States sailors wear their insignia designating rank—right or left?

269. What are "krill"?

265. OLIVER WENDELL HOLMES.

266. IT WAS DESTROYED WHILE IN STORAGE IN A SHED IN ANNAPOLIS DURING THE PALM SUNDAY BLIZZARD OF 1944. THE SHED COLLAPSED ON TOP OF IT AND OBLITERATED THE YACHT THAT WAS VIRTUALLY SYNONYMOUS WITH INTERNATIONAL YACHT RACING.

267. BETWEEN THE VESSEL AND A DOCK, TO ACT AS A SORT OF FENDER.

268. SAILORS WEAR THEIR ENSIGNIA ON THE LEFT SIDE.

269. TINY SHRIMPLIKE CREATURES WHICH WHALES EAT.

270. What name was Western Cruise Line's *Azure Seas* originally christened by Queen Elizabeth II in 1955?

271. Who wrote *Billy Budd, Sailor?*

272. How high is a "killer wave"?
   1. 50 feet.
   2. 75 feet.
   3. 100 feet.

273. In naval jargon what does "give it the deep six" mean?

274. A "dugong" and a "manatee" are types of _______ ______ .

270.   THE *SOUTHERN CROSS.*

271.   HERMAN MELVILLE.

272.   #3.   100 FEET HIGH.

273.   TO HEAVE OVERBOARD OR PERMANENTLY DISCARD.

274.   SEA COWS. THE SEA COW OF THE WESTERN PACIFIC IS CALLED A DUGONG AND THE SEA COWS OF THE FLORIDA RIVERS ARE MANATEES. THE MANATEE IS IN DANGER OF BECOMING EXTINCT.

275. What and where is the tallest brick lighthouse in America?

276. Are there any descendants of Fletcher Christian (mutineer of the *Bounty*) still alive and, if so, where do they live?

277. What body of water (located in the southwest part of the United States) surrounded by canyons was used for the background of "Planet of the Apes"?

278. What is the common name for the largest whale in the sea?

279. What is the animal name given to the last man on the academic grade list at the U.S. Naval Academy?

275. CAPE HATTERAS LIGHTHOUSE IS 190 FEET — LOCATED IN NORTH CAROLINA.

276. YES. THE GREAT-GREAT-GRANDSON OF FLETCHER CHRISTIAN AND *HIS* DESCENDANTS, LIVE ON PITCAIRN ISLAND, MIDWAY BETWEEN PANAMA AND NEW ZEALAND.

277. LAKE POWELL ON THE UTAH - ARIZONA BORDER.

278. BLUE WHALE. THE MALE MAY BE MORE THAN 100 FEET LONG AND WEIGH NEARLY 200 TONS.

279. THE GOAT.

280. Who said about Cunard officers, "Cunard people would not take Noah himself until they had worked him up through all the lower grades and tried him ten years"?
1. Mark Twain
2. Captain Robert Arnott
3. William H. Flayhart III
4. Walter Lord

281. The galley smoke pipe on a vessel is referred to by a man's name. What is it called?

282. A type of so-called pirates derive their name from the French word for "a drier of beef." What group is this?

283. In what year did *Queen Mary* cease being a ship and become a building?

280.   MARK TWAIN.

281.   CHARLIE NOBLE.

282.   THE *BUCCANEERS. Boucanier* is the French word for a "drier of beef" — the West Indies Islands were overrun with cattle, especially San Domingo. When the Spaniards heard of this trading in beef within the environs of their territory, they pursued the ships that the buccaneers sailed and tried relentlessly to destroy them. Gradually a state of maritime warfare developed between the two factions. The outside world started calling "The Brethren of the Coast" buccaneers and pirates.

283.   1967.

284. What is the combination of rum mixed with water called?

285. To "dance, and promenade, and smoke, and sing, and make love, and search the skies for constellations—that's what people expect of a cruise," wrote Mark Twain. In what book did Mark Twain record his experiences on an 1860's Middle East cruise?

286. Why was there only a minimal number of candles on Vasco da Gama's flagship *São Gabriel?*

287. How many sailors, who did *not* join the mutineers, chose to go in the launch with Captain Bligh?

284. GROG. THIS TERM CAME FROM "OLD GROG," THE NICK-NAME OF EDWARD VERNON, AN ADMIRAL RESPONSIBLE FOR DILUTING SAILOR'S RUM. A DASH OF LEMON AND SUGAR IS SOMETIMES ADDED TO HEATED GROG.

285. *THE INNOCENTS ABROAD.* HE CALLED HIS OWN EXPERIENCE "A FUNERAL WITHOUT A CORPSE."

286. BECAUSE THE SHIP WAS MADE OF WOOD AND FIRE WAS ALWAYS A THREAT. THEREFORE, THERE WAS ONLY "A CANDLE FOR THE MASTER AND ONE FOR THE COMPASS."

287. 18.

288. What was the name of the ship on which the naturalist and author Charles Darwin (who wrote *Origin of Species*) sailed in 1832?

289. What kind of clothing did the figurehead of Captain Bligh's *Bounty* wear?

290. What novel by Victor Hugo has the word "Sea" in its title?

291. Who was the master of the *Golden Hind?*

292. What is the purpose of a "lazarette" on a boat?

288.   H.M.S. *BEAGLE.*

289.   THE FIGUREHEAD WAS OF A WOMAN IN A RIDING HABIT.

290.   *TOILERS OF THE SEA.*

291.   FRANCIS DRAKE, WHO WAS KNIGHTED "SIR" AND CALLED "DEARE PYRAT" BY QUEEN ELIZABETH.

292.   A "LAZARETTE" IS A SPACE FOR STOWAGE IN A BOAT'S STERN.

293. The Apollo 15 astronauts named their command spacecraft in honor of Captain Cook's ship. What was the name of Cook's vessel?

294. The "Herreshoff brothers of Bristol" (Rhode Island) were most noted for being which of the following:
1. Ship captains.
2. Boat builders.
3. Pirates.

295. What is the name of the marine insurance organization that started out as a coffee house?

296. Is the gold decoration on a naval officer's uniform correctly called "gold lace" or "gold braid"?

293.　　*ENDEAVOUR.*

294.　　#2.　BOAT BUILDERS. John and Nathanael Herreshoff owned a boatbuilding company that built some of the finest yachts in the world. James, the eldest Herreshoff brother, was an inventor. The yachts *Constitution* and *Reliance* were two of many boats produced at the Herreshoffs' plant.

295.　　LLOYD'S OF LONDON.

296.　　GOLD LACE.

297. What was the name of the first ship in history to rest on the surface of the Arctic Ocean at the North Pole?

298. A hovercraft is also called an "S.E.S." What do these initials stand for?

299. The *Nautilus,* the first atomic-powered sub in the U.S. Navy, was decommissioned in 1980, and in 1985 was towed from Mare Island, California to an eastern harbor. Where did it end up, and what happened to it?

300. What liner, currently cruising, has the most teak, brass and glass in its structure?

297. U.S.S. *SKATE* — MARCH OF 1979.

298. SURFACE — EFFECT SHIPS.

299. THE *NAUTILUS* ENDED UP IN GROTON, CONNECTICUT WHERE IT IS NOW A MUSEUM.

300. THE *ROYAL PRINCESS.*

Queen Mary
(Courtesy of the Long Beach Press-Telegram
Michael Rondou—1985).

Pismo Beach Friends
by author.

Texas Light
(Courtesy of Dick Daugird).

Gibbs Hill Lighthouse, East Chop Light and Gay Head Light.
Photos by author.

Queen Elizabeth at Cherbourg, *Berengaria* and the *Normandie*
(Courtesy of Eric Sauder collection).

QE2 in port by author
and
QE2 at night (Courtesy of Ken Marschall).

The *Olympic, Mauretania,* and *Lusitania*
(Courtesy of Ken Marschall collection).

Eva Hart, Ruth Blanchard and Marshall Drew
author's collection.

Nancy Brown and the S.S. *Norway*.
Photos by author.

"The Breakers", Newport, Rhode Island and the
smallest drawbridge in the world.
Photos by author.

Sea Silhouette by author
and
The *Star of India*
(Courtesy of the San Diego Convention and Visitors Bureau).

"Squareriggers."
Photos by author at South Street Museum, New York
and at Nassau.

142

Watercolor by Doug Cable.
Oil Painting of the Queen Elizabeth 2 by Robin Davies
done on board in 1983 for use as a Christmas card.
(Courtesy of Robin Davies, Food and Beverage Manager
of the *Queen Elizabeth 2*).

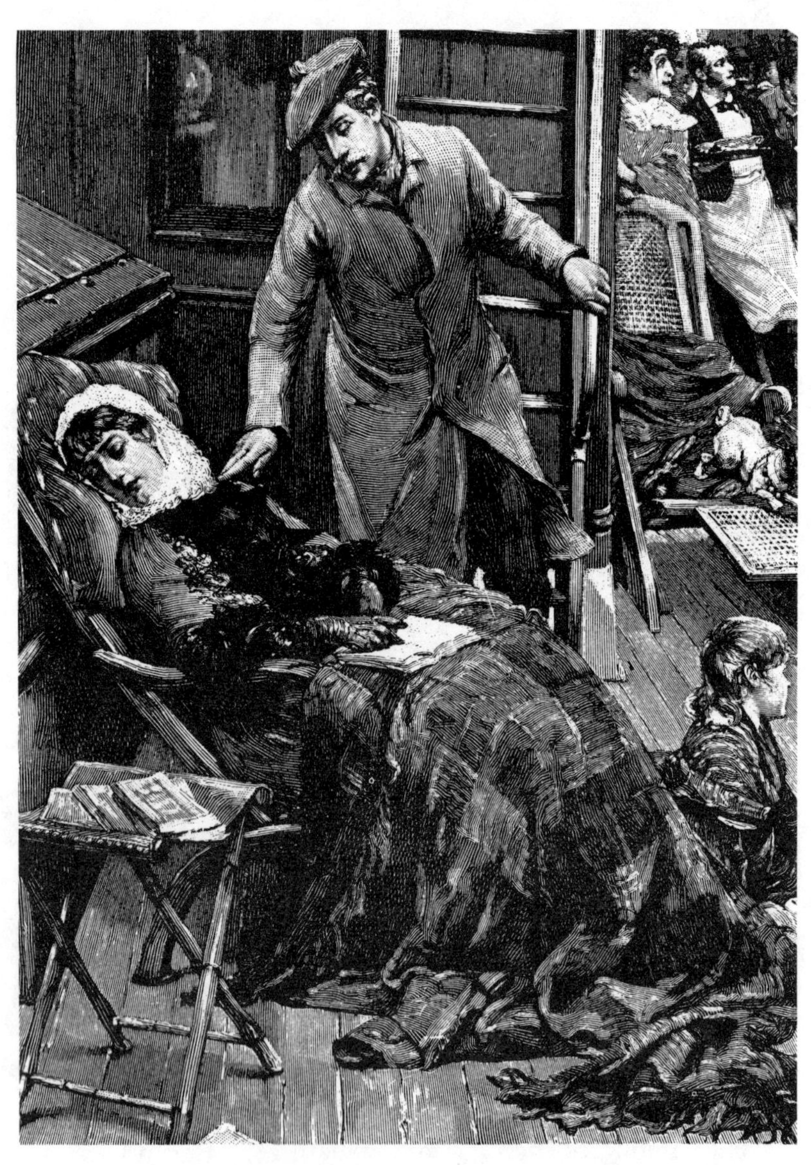

"Wake up dear, it is time for more Mariner's Trivia."

301. What is the name of the space aboard a ship or liner which is a messroom assigned to officers?

302. What steamboat is now a museum in Shelburne, Vermont?

303. What is the job of a ship's "pilot"?

304. What does the expression "He let the cat out of the bag" have to do with early traditions of the sea?

305. What is the largest island in San Francisco Bay?

301.   WARD ROOM.

302.   *TICONDEROGA.*

303.   A PILOT IS A PERSON WHO IS QUALIFIED (AND USUALLY LICENSED) TO CONDUCT A SHIP INTO AND OUT OF A PORT OR SPECIFIED WATERS.

304.   ON THE SQUARE RIGGERS SAILORS WERE PUNISHED BY A FLOGGING WITH A CAT-OF-NINE-TAILS WHICH WAS KEPT IN A CANVAS BAG.

305.   ANGEL ISLAND. FROM 1850 TO 1853 THE STATE ANCHORED SHIPS' HULKS OFF THE ISLAND AND JAILED PRISONERS IN THEM.

306. Five yachts of Sir Thomas Lipton were given the same name. They sailed in five America's Cup races and never won the "auld mug." What were the names of the yachts?

307. Why should a ship's officer arrive five minutes ahead of time for his night watch on the bridge?

308. What was the name of the famous sea captain in C.S. Forester's books?

309. What was the name of the pirate-slave-treasure ship whose master was Samuel (Black) Bellamy? (It sank with Bellamy aboard off the coast of Cape Cod in 1717.)

306.   *SHAMROCK.*

307.   BEING FIVE MINUTES EARLY WILL GIVE A PERSON'S EYES
        A CHANCE TO GET ACCUSTOMED TO DARKNESS.

308.   CAPTAIN HORATIO HORNBLOWER.

309.   *WHIDAH.*

310. What was the name of the battle, in May of 1942, which was the first naval engagement in history when surface vessels did not exchange a single shot?

311. What aspiring Roman politician was captured by pirates in 81 B.C. while cruising the Mediterranean?

312. There is an old saying that pouring "oil on troubled waters" can calm a rough sea. Is this true or an old wive's tale?

313. Who said, "Fire when ready, Mr. Gridley"?

314. What does it mean when you see printed on an Admiralty navigation chart the letters "E.D." or "P.D." near the location of islands in the sea?

310.   THE BATTLE OF THE CORAL SEA, WITH CARRIER PLANES STRIKING AT JAPANESE WARSHIPS.

311.   JULIUS CAESAR. He later had his abductors captured and literally crucified. He was especially thoughtful of certain members of the pirate gang who had treated him nicely — he had them killed *before* they were nailed to the crosses.

312.   IT IS *TRUE* THAT OIL HAS A CALMING EFFECT ON A ROUGH SEA. Oil prevents the breaking of waves and sometimes even prevents them from forming. Animal and vegetable oils are supposedly the best.

313.   ADMIRAL GEORGE DEWEY.

314.   THESE ARE "DOUBTFUL ISLANDS," DISTINGUISHED BY THE SKEPTICAL "EXISTENCE DOUBTFUL" OR "POSITION DOUBTFUL." ISLANDS HAVE BEEN REPORTED IN GOOD FAITH THAT IN ACTUALITY TURNED OUT TO BE NON-EXISTENT.

315. What author wrote "The Liner she's a lady"?

316. If your boat capsizes or swamps, is it better to swim to shore (if in sight) or to stay with the boat?

317. How is the saying "everything is aboveboard" (which in our vernacular means "honest") supposedly linked to piracy?

318. How many sailing junks are, as of this writing, registered in Hong Kong?
1. None
2. 1,525
3. 9,889

319. What did Mercator do in 1569 that added utility and clarity to mapmaking?

315.   RUDYARD KIPLING.

316.   TO STAY WITH THE BOAT. THE SHORE ALWAYS LOOKS CLOSER THAN IT IS.

317.   IT IS THOUGHT TO HAVE BEEN LINKED TO THE PIRATE PRACTICE OF HIDING CREWS BELOW DECKS TO ENTICE MERCHANT SHIPS TO COME CLOSE.

318.   #1.   NONE. According to marine historians Neil Hollander and Harold Mertes (authors of *The Last Sailors*) not a single sailing junk is registered in Hong Kong. The mainland is the homeland of the remaining junks, and junks are becoming extinct.

319.   HE PRODUCED THE FIRST CHART OF THE WORLD IN WHICH THE SPHERICAL SHAPE OF THE EARTH IS TRANSLATED INTO A FLAT SURFACE IN SUCH A MANNER AS TO MAKE PLOTTING A COURSE BETWEEN TWO POINTS EASIER.

320. Who wrote the haunting: "I was a child and she was a child, in this kingdom by the sea"?

321. What does the acronym SCUBA stand for?

322. What does the figurehead on Britain's *Cutty Sark* have in her outstretched hand?

323. What is "sea-otter's cabbage"?

324. To what division of the Navy does a Seabee belong and exactly what does a Seabee do?

320.   EDGAR ALLAN POE IN A POEM ENTITLED "ANNABEL LEE."

321.   SELF-CONTAINED UNDERWATER BREATHING APPARATUS.

322.   A MARE'S TAIL.

323.   A GIGANTIC KELP OF THE NORTHERN PACIFIC.

324.   A SEABEE (STANDS FOR C.B.) IS A MEMBER OF THE U.S. NAVY'S CONSTRUCTION BATTALION AND BUILDS NAVAL SHORE FACILITIES IN COMBAT ZONES.

325. In the old days, why did British sailors wear black kerchiefs around their necks?

326. In symbolism, do the Chinese believe that waves are the abode of dragons or that they are symbolic of purity, or both?

327. In Lewis Carroll's *Through The Looking-Glass* who said that the time had come to talk "of shoes and ships—and sealing wax—"?

328. What is the difference between a ship and a boat?

329. Is the "sea robin" a bird, fish or sea urchin?

325.   TO KEEP THEIR TARRED PIGTAILS FROM SOILING THEIR UNIFORMS.

326.   BOTH.

327.   THE WALRUS.

328.   A BOAT CAN BE CARRIED ON A SHIP — THE EXCEPTION BEING A SUBMARINE, WHICH IS REFERRED TO AS A BOAT.

329.   A FISH OF THE TRIGLIDAE FAMILY.

330. What was the name of the vessel in *Twenty Thousand Leagues Under the Sea* (by Jules Verne) that was sent to investigate the phenomenon of the *Nautilus?*

331. Why are helmsmen careful not to carry steel pocket-knives when at the wheel of a vessel?

332. What is "lagan"?

333. In what harbor did the battleship *Maine* blow up in 1898?

334. In mythology, who was the trumpeter of the sea who used a great shell?

330.   THE *ABRAHAM LINCOLN*.

331.   STEEL AND IRON CAUSE ERRORS IN COMPASSES. FERROUS METALS ATTRACT THE MAGNETIZED NEEDLE IN A COMPASS CAUSING IT TO DEFECT.

332.   JETTISONED GOODS SUNK AT SEA AND MARKED BY A BUOY FOR INTENDED RECOVERY.

333.   HAVANA HARBOR IN CUBA. IN APRIL OF 1898 THE U.S. DECLARED WAR ON SPAIN.

334.   TRITON.

335. It is not widely known, but the expression "blue Monday" has a nautical background. Where did it originate?

336. What is the name of the fixed line on the compass of a ship that is aligned with the longitudinal axis of the ship?

337. During the time of Columbus a device known as The Dutchman's Log was used on ships. What was its purpose?

338. Who wrote, "There is no Frigate like a Book to Take us Lands away"?

339. What is the name of the fiery emanations that are sometimes seen at the tips of a ship's mast or spar?

335. IN THE DAYS OF SQUARE RIGGERS A SAILOR'S MISDEEDS WERE WRITTEN DOWN DAILY, BUT THE PUNISHMENTS FOR THESE SO-CALLED CRIMES WEREN'T CARRIED OUT UNTIL THE FOLLOWING MONDAY; THUS, "BLUE MONDAY."

336. LUBBER LINE.

337. TO FIND OUT THE SPEED OF A SHIP, A SUBSTANCE OR OBJECT (SUCH AS A WOODEN LOG OR STICK) WHICH WOULD FLOAT LIGHTLY ON THE WATER WAS THROWN OVER THE SIDE OF THE SHIP. THE TIME IT TOOK THIS TO PASS TWO MEN SPACED AT A KNOWN DISTANCE APART GAVE AN ESTIMATE OF SPEED.

338. EMILY DICKINSON.

339. ST. ELMO'S FIRE. THE ONLY EXPLANATION SEEMS TO BE THAT THIS PHENOMENON IS DUE TO UNIQUE WEATHER CONDITIONS.

340.   Who had "the face that launched a thousand ships"?

341.   How did the term "scuttlebutt" originate?

342.   What did the "sirens" look like, whose beautiful singing lured sailors to their deaths?

343.   What is a more common name for "hardtack"?

344.   The Panama Canal may at times have more *large* ships passing through than any other, but there is another canal that is the *busiest* overall, with traffic ranging from small sailboats to supertankers—is it the Kiel or the Suez?

340.   HELEN OF TROY — SHE INDIRECTLY STARTED THE TROJAN
        WAR.

341.   THE NAVY SUPPLIED CASKS OF FRESH WATER FOR SAI-
        LORS TO DRINK FROM AND WHILE GATHERED AT THESE
        CASKS THE SAILORS WOULD PAUSE TO EXCHANGE GOS-
        SIP AND RUMORS. THE DICTIONARY DEFINES SCUTTLE AS
        A DRINKING BOWL.

342.   SINCE NO ONE WHO SAW THEM EVER RETURNED, WHAT
        THEY LOOKED LIKE IS NOT KNOWN.

343.   BREAD OR BISCUIT. HARDTACK IS A SALTLESS HARD BIS-
        CUIT OR BREAD MADE OF FLOUR AND WATER, SOMETIMES
        CALLED SEA BREAD.

344.   THE KIEL AT HOLTENAU, WEST GERMANY JUST NORTH
        OF KIEL ON THE BALTIC SEA. MORE THAN 90,000 SHIPS
        PASS THROUGH EACH YEAR.

345. What is the unique distinction of Bouvet Island (owned by Norway)?

346. From what hymn are these lines taken? "Oh hear us when we cry to Thee, For those in peril on the sea."

347. What is another name for the small smelt fish that spawn on the sandy beach of California during the high tides of March through June?

348. In Navy jargon, what does the small letter "z" stand for when referring to weather conditions?

345.   IT IS THE MOST ISOLATED UNINHABITED SPOT IN THE WHOLE WORLD. ONE CAN DRAW A CIRCLE OF A 1,000 MILE RADIUS IN WHICH THERE IS NO OTHER LAND.

346.   "ETERNAL FATHER STRONG TO SAVE."

347.   GRUNION.

348.   HAZY.

349. Mel Fisher is the name of the man who discovered the hulk of the 17th-century Spanish galleon (*Nuestra Señora de Atocha*) with as much as 400 million dollars worth of treasure on board. Off the coast of what state was this discovery made?

350. In Navy terminology what is a "Field Day"?

351. How many feet wide are the locks to accommodate barges in the rivers of England?
1. 12 feet.
2. 14 feet.
3. 24 feet.

352. Who said, "If a man doesn't know to what port he is steering, no wind is favorable to him"? Was it Seneca, Shakespere, Twain, or Emerson?

349.   FLORIDA.

350.   A DAY FOR GENERAL CLEANING.

351.   #1. 12 FEET WIDE.

352.   SENECA.

353. A seacock is which of the following:
   1. An ocean bird.
   2. A shutoff valve for pipes.
   3. A type of sea urchin.

354. A cockleshell is both a seashell and a light flimsy boat—true or false?

355. In olden days what did a flag with the letter "G" flown from the mast of a boat indicate?

356. There are two types of compasses: dry and wet. Which is most prevalent in American ships?

357. Will water put out a gasoline fire on a boat?

353.   A SHUTOFF VALVE ATTACHED TO THROUGH-HULL PIPES.

354.   TRUE.

355.   THAT THE BOAT WANTED THEIR GARBAGE PICKED UP.

356.   WET, OR MARINER'S COMPASS.

357.   NO, YOU NEED TO HAVE A FIRE EXTINGUISHER.

358. What author who sailed from almost one end of the globe to the other wrote *The Sea Wolf?*

359. What or who in the coastal town of Whitby, England, is known as the "Whitby mad bull"?

360. What do whales eat the first six or seven months of their lives?

361. In nautical terms what does "the cut of one's jib" mean?

362. What time in the morning should colors (flags) be raised on a ship?

358. JACK LONDON.

359. THE POWERFUL *FOG SIREN* LOCATED NEAR HIGH LIGHT-HOUSE ON A 240-FOOT CLIFF.

360. MILK. WHALES ARE MAMMALS. AFTER SIX MONTHS THEY EAT PLANKTON.

361. ONE'S APPEARANCE.

362. 8:00 IN THE MORNING. THE FLAG IS TAKEN DOWN AT SUNDOWN.

363. What two things did "The Owl and the Pussycat" take to sea in their pea-green boat?

364. On what island is the world's smallest drawbridge located?

365. After whom were the Chesapeake Bay ferries usually named?

366. What ship had a real carousel in the children's playroom?

367. Are the rules for navigational lights of sea planes the same as for seagoing vessels?

363.   HONEY AND PLENTY OF MONEY.

364.   BERMUDA. THE "DRAW" IS AN 18-INCH WOODEN FLAP IN THE CENTER OF THE BRIDGE TO ACCOMMODATE A SAIL-BOAT'S MAST.

365.   MARYLAND GOVERNORS. *GOVERNOR HARRINGTON*, FOR EXAMPLE.

366.   THE *ILE DE FRANCE.*

367.   YES.

368. Was there ever an actual case of a man being swallowed by a whale and living, or is Jonah's tale fictional?

369. A bell tolls at Lloyd's of London when a ship is lost. What is this bell called?

370. Mark Twain said, "You go to heaven if you want—I'll stay right here." What island was he talking about?

371. What sailor/actor (at one time married to Madeleine Carroll) wrote a book called *Wanderer* about his life at sea?

372. What "first" was the nuclear submarine U.S.S. *Triton* commended for in 1960?

368.   YES, THERE WAS AN ACTUAL CASE. In 1891 an English sailor named James Bartley, who worked as a harpooner, was thought drowned after a huge whale capsized his boat. Bartley was found unconscious the following day when the whale's stomach was cut open. Needless to say, Bartley was never quite the same and his face, neck and hands remained white from the whale's gastric juices the rest of his life.

369.   THE LUTINE BELL.

370.   BERMUDA.

371.   STERLING HAYDEN.

372.   SHE COMPLETED THE FIRST SUBMERGED CIRCUMNAVI-GATION OF THE GLOBE IN SIXTY DAYS. HER CAPTAIN WAS EDWARD BEACH.

373. Where is the oldest cast iron lighthouse in the world located?

374. According to mythology, what did the sacrilegious sinner Ajax boast of that prompted Poseidon to cause his death?

375. Besides being ugly to look at, what else is wrong with parrot fish?

376. What ship was referred to as the "cheesebox on a raft"?

373.   HAMILTON, BERMUDA. IT IS CALLED GIBB'S LIGHTHOUSE.

374.   AJAX SAID HE WAS ONE PERSON THE SEA COULD NOT DROWN, AND ARROGANCE ALWAYS AROUSED THE ANGER OF THE GODS.

375.   THEY ARE POISONOUS TO EAT.

376.   THE *MONITOR*.

377. Lighthouse keeper William Williams explained how a "boon," or barrel of provisions, was kept on a rock island in the late 17th century until a lighthouse was established in 1811. Off the coast of what state is Boon Island located?

378. What writer predicted that we would have atomic submarines long before they were a reality?

379. What ship (still sailing) in olden days had the most spacious and beautiful library afloat?

380. What island is Britain's oldest colony?

381. Is it truth or fiction that the liner *QE2* was ever in danger of terrorists' attack?

377.   MAINE.

378.   JULES VERNE.

379.   "QE2." THE ROOM WAS LATER DISMANTLED AND CON-
VERTED TO HOLD SLOT MACHINES.

380.   BERMUDA.

381.   TRUTH. Colonel Muammar Qaddafi is reported to have ordered
an Egyptian submarine to torpedo the *QE2*. Anwar Sadat (who
was President of Egypt) upon hearing of the dictator's orders,
recalled the submarine and managed to avoid a disaster.

382. What Oakland, California writer spent time both in jail and as a member of the harbor police? He was a sailor and owned a sloop.

383. Tidal waves are caused by:
1. Movement of the ocean floor.
2. Tides.

384. Lord Nelson, whose death came at the moment of victory in the battle of Trafalgar, asked a favor of his flag captain. Nelson's dying words were: "Now I am satisfied—thank God I have done my duty." Just before that what did he request that his flag captain, Thomas Hardy, do?

385. What Secretary of Treasury called Cape Hatteras the "Graveyard of the Atlantic" and was instrumental in having a lighthouse built there?

382.   JACK LONDON.

383.   #1.   MOVEMENT OF THE OCEAN FLOOR. TIDAL WAVES
ARE ALSO CALLED SEISMIC SEA WAVES.

384.   NELSON ASKED HARDY TO BESTOW A KISS UPON HIS
CHEEK. NELSON WAS MORE THAN A TACTICALLY BRIL-
LIANT COMMANDER; HE WAS A BELOVED LEADER OF MEN
AND TRUSTED BY BOTH COMMON SEAMEN AND HIS
OFFICERS.

385.   ALEXANDER HAMILTON.

386. What famous yacht race is fondly referred to as the "thrash to the Onion Patch"?

387. What U.S. battleship is credited with firing both the first and last 16-inch salvos of World War II?

388. What pirate (one of the nastiest) stuck smoldering matches under his hat to look more frightful?

*

389. Do two short blasts from a ship's whistle mean that you are altering your course to the port side or starboard?

386.   NEWPORT, RHODE ISLAND, TO BERMUDA.

387.   U.S.S. *MASSACHUSETTS*, IN THE INVASION OF NORTH AFRICA IN 1942 AND THE BOMBARDMENT OF JAPAN IN 1945. SHE RESIDES NOW IN FALL RIVER, MASSACHUSETTS.

388.   BLACKBEARD.

389.   PORT, OR LEFT.

390. Which of the signals listed below indicates a ship in distress?
1. A gun fired at intervals of about a minute.
2. An S.O.S. by Morse code.
3. A rocket fired, with red or white stars fired one at a time.

391. When reading flag signals, from which position are the flags of a hoisting of the colors read?
1. the top down.
2. the bottom up.

392. In the oldest drydock in the world can be seen the oldest vessel on the British Naval List, H.M.S. *Victory*. Where is this drydock?

393. The weight of fuel, fresh water, ballast, stores, cargo, passengers and crew is called "dead weight"—true or false?

390.   ALL, #1, #2, AND #3.

391.   #1. THE TOP DOWN.

392.   PORTSMOUTH, ENGLAND.

393.   TRUE.

394. What lighthouse in California was under the care of female attendants for forty years?

395. What words come after Kipling's "Come you back to Mandalay, Where the _______ _______ _______"?

396. What are "jigger" and "mizzen"?

397. In a U.S. Navy standard magnetic compass what liquids are in the bowl of the compass?

398. What does "pratique" mean?

394.   POINT PINOS LIGHTHOUSE (ON A POINT AT THE SOUTH
        SIDE OF THE ENTRANCE TO MONTEREY BAY).

395.   —OLD FLOTILLA LAY."

396.   MASTS ON SAILING SHIPS.

397.   MIXTURE OF ALCOHOL AND DISTILLED WATER, WHICH
        WILL NOT FREEZE.

398.   CLEARANCE GIVEN AN INCOMING SHIP BY THE HEALTH
        AUTHORITY OF A PORT.

399. What was so unusual about the ship called the *Thomas W. Lawson?*

400. What do the names Eva Hart, Marshall Drew and Ruth Blanchard have in common?

401. What were the colors used on the funnels of the Holland America Line?

402. Name one object, person or animal, pictured on the Coat of Arms of Trinity House (the organization which controls lighthouses around the coast of England and Wales).

403. What ship was nicknamed the "Grey Ghost"?

399.   SHE WAS THE ONLY SEVEN-MASTED SAILING VESSEL
        EVER BUILT.

400.   ALL ARE SURVIVORS OF THE *TITANIC* AND STILL LIVING
        AT THE TIME THIS BOOK WAS PUBLISHED.

401.   GREEN, YELLOW AND WHITE.

402.   THE COAT OF ARMS CONTAINS A *SHIELD* WITH FOUR *SAIL-
        ING SHIPS,* AND AT THE TOP IS A CROWNED *LION* BRAN-
        DISHING A *SWORD.*

403.   *QUEEN MARY,* DURING HER GREY-PAINTED TROOPING
        YEARS IN WORLD WAR II.

404. When a person decides to give up seafaring and settle ashore, the slang way of saying this is "He's swallowing the __________ ."

405. If a Coast Guard person told you that any time you go out on your boat you should have a PFD with you, to what would he or she be referring?

406. What was the nickname of the device which protected the *Queen Mary* and the *Queen Elizabeth* from acoustic mines and torpedoes?

407. The *Falls of Clyde* built in Scotland in 1878 has gradually been restored as a full-rigged ship. In the waters of what city and state is she now berthed?

404. "HE'S SWALLOWING THE ANCHOR."

405. PFD REFERS TO "PERSONAL FLOTATION DEVICE." YOU NEED ONE THAT WILL KEEP YOUR AIRWAYS FREE OF WATER IN CASE YOU ARE UNCONSCIOUS.

406. "BRASS BANDS." MOUNTED IN THE FORWARD HULL, THEY SENT OUT SOUND WAVES CAUSING MINES OR TORPEDOES TO EXPLODE AT A DISTANCE.

407. THE *FALLS OF CLYDE* IS AT PIER 5, HONOLULU HARBOR IN HAWAII.

408. What two great shipping companies merged in July of 1934?

409. What is the name of the southernmost extremity in Cornwall, England that can be seen from the sea and is named after a reptile?

410. What is the largest man-made small-craft harbor in the world?

411. What is the principal cargo of a Great Lakes freighter?

412. Does SOS really stand for anything?

408.   THE CUNARD AND WHITE STAR LINES.

409.   THE LIZARD.

410.   MARINA DEL REY, CALIFORNIA.

411.   IRON ORE.

412.   IT DOESN'T STAND FOR SAVE OUR SOULS OR SAVE OUR SHIP OR ANYTHING. IT WAS ORIGINALLY SELECTED BECAUSE OF ITS SIMPLICITY TO TRANSMIT: THREE DOTS, THREE DASHES, PLUS THREE DOTS.

413. What ship was nicknamed "Rolling Billy"?

414. What tonnage do Biblical records fix for Noah's
      Ark?
      1. 20,000 tons.
      2. 40,000 tons.
      3. 60,000 tons.

415. Who wrote a poem in which a character named
      Tam calls out: "well done, cutty sark" to a charm-
      ing witch who dances enchantingly and can outrun
      the wind?

416. What does it mean when a ship is seen entering
      port with a broom hanging from her mast?

413.   *KAISER WILHELM DER GROSSE.*

414.   20,000 TONS.

415.   ROBERT BURNS — THE SHIP *CUTTY SARK* DERIVED ITS NAME FROM THIS POEM ABOUT A WITCH WHO DANCED IN A SHORT SKIRT (OR PETTICOAT).

416.   IT MEANS THAT SHE HAS BROKEN A SPEED RECORD, "SWEEPING" AWAY THE COMPETITION.

417. When a bottle of champagne shatters on a ship's bow at a launching, what does the liquid symbolically represent?

418. What club designed the "yacht ensign" flag that has the traditional 13 stripes and a fouled anchor surrounded by 13 stars?

419. What was innovative about the lighting in the ballroom of the *Queen Mary?*

420. What pirate fought against the British in the Battle of New Orleans (1815)?

421. Why does May 7, 1915, stand out in maritime history?

417. BLOOD. IN ANCIENT TIMES SACRIFICIAL ANIMAL HEADS WERE PLACED ON THE PROW AT LAUNCHING TO PLACATE THE DANGEROUS WATERS.

418. THE NEW YORK YACHT CLUB.

419. IT HAD A SYSTEM OF COLORED LIGHTS WHICH VARIED ACCORDING TO THE MUSIC.

420. JEAN LAFFITE. LAFFITE WAS PARDONED FOR HIS PREVIOUS WICKED WAYS BY PRESIDENT MADISON. IT IS SAID THAT LAFFITE'S PENITENT ATTITUDE WAS SHORTLIVED.

421. IT WAS THE DAY THE GERMAN SUBMARINE U-20 FIRED A TORPEDO INTO THE *LUSITANIA*, SENDING HER TO THE BOTTOM IN ONLY 18 MINUTES, WITH A LOSS OF OVER 1200 LIVES.

422. When a triangular red flag is flying from a yacht club or a Coast Guard station, what does this indicate?

423. What United States aircraft carrier has been turned into a memorial and is on display in New York City?

424. What was the name of Aristotle Onassis' yacht?

425. Were more passenger ships lost in World War I or World War II?

426. Grace Darling (1815-1842) is a heroine to the English people. What did she do that was to earn her honors?

422. THAT PARTICULAR FLAG'S TITLE IS "SMALL CRAFT WARN-ING" AND SHOULD BE TAKEN LITERALLY.

423. THE U.S.S. *INTREPID*.

424. *CHRISTINA*.

425. WORLD WAR I.

426. SHE (ALONG WITH HER FATHER WILLIAM DARLING WHO WAS LIGHTKEEPER OF THE LONGSTONE, FARNE ISLANDS LIGHTHOUSE) SAVED NINE PEOPLE FROM DROWNING WHEN THE *FORFARSHIRE* WAS WRECKED WITH THE LOSS OF 43 PERSONS. THEY RECEIVED THE GOLD MEDAL FROM THE HUMANE SOCIETY FOR THEIR GALLANT EFFORTS.

427. During the Second World War, what two ships sailed over a million miles and carried about two million service personnel?

428. Where is (or *was*, by the time you read this) the 1987 America's Cup race held?

429. From where to where is the "longest race" (of 3,571 miles) for yachts conducted?

430. What did steamer-trunk stickers "Not wanted on voyage" mean?

431. In the old saying, "between the devil and the deep blue sea" what, in nautical terms, does the devil mean?

427.   THE *QUEEN MARY* AND THE *QUEEN ELIZABETH*.

428.   PERTH, AUSTRALIA.

429.   THE TRANSPACIFIC EVENT IS FROM LOS ANGELES TO TAHITI.

430.   THESE TRUNKS COULD BE STORED IN THE HOLD. THERE WAS NO NEED FOR THE CONTENTS DURING THE VOYAGE.

431.   THE "DEVIL" IS THE SEAM IN A WOODEN SHIP'S HULL RIGHT DOWN NEXT TO THE WATERLINE AND IS "THE DEVIL" TO GET AT WHEN CALKING OR PAINTING. THUS THERE IS A VERY SMALL MARGIN BETWEEN THE DEVIL AND THE SEA. IN DAILY LANGUAGE THE TERM MEANS TO BE IN A DIFFICULT OR TIGHT SPOT.

432. What is the "citadel" in a battleship?

433. Why is Berth 108 in Southampton "death row" for ships?

434. The Blue Ribbon is flown from the mast of a ship upon breaking a speed record. True or false?

435. What is composer Claude Debussy's work called that has the word "sea" in the title? Hint: It is in French.

436. What is a transatlantic ocean voyage called?

432. *AN ARMORED BOX* SURROUNDING THE INTERIOR WHICH CONTAINS MACHINERY SPACES, AMMUNITION MAGAZINES AND VITAL CONTROL EQUIPMENT. THE SIDES OF THIS PROTECTIVE STEEL ARMOR ARE 11 TO 16 INCHES THICK.

433. THAT'S WHERE THEY ARE DOCKED BEFORE THEY GO TO THE WRECKERS TO BE SCRAPPED.

434. FALSE; THE BLUE RIBBON IS ONLY A MYTHICAL SYMBOL. HOWEVER, THE HALE'S TROPHY, GIVEN FOR THE FASTEST CROSSING, IS REAL.

435. "LA MER."

436. A "CROSSING."

437. What term is used to describe the condition where nitrogen in a diver's body tissue dissolves into his or her blood?

438. What was the most common hour for liner departures from New York before World War II?

439. Why, in 1767, did Captain Samuel Wallis of the *Dolphin* forbid his crew members to go on shore leave until they confessed that they were stealing nails from his ship?

440. What was the first ship to include a synagogue in her design?

441. What was the ultimate fate of the liner *Paris?*

437.   THE "BENDS."

438.   MIDNIGHT.

439.   BECAUSE THE MAINSAIL OF HIS SHIP (THE *DOLPHIN*) COL-
        LAPSED IN TAHITI. YOUNG TAHITIAN GIRLS GAVE SEXUAL
        FAVORS TO CREWMEMBERS IN RETURN FOR IRON NAILS,
        WHICH WERE A RARE COMMODITY. THE NATIVES USED
        THE IRON NAILS FOR FISH HOOKS AND BORING HOLES IN
        THE PLANKS OF CANOES.

440.   THE *QUEEN MARY*, 1936.

441.   THE *PARIS* WAS A VICTIM OF A PIERSIDE FIRE.

442. A Chinese seaman named Poon Lim managed to survive aboard a small raft after the ship he served on (S.S. *Ben Lomond*) was torpedoed by a German submarine during World War II. How long was he on the raft before he was picked up fully conscious and still able to walk?
1. 21 days.
2. 36 days.
3. 133 days.

443. How fast can bottlenose dolphins swim?
1. 15 miles per hour.
2. 75 miles per hour.
3. 25 miles per hour.

444. What do the letters HIN stand for in boating registration?

442.   #3.   133 DAYS.

443.   #3.   25 MILES PER HOUR.

444.   HULL IDENTIFICATION NUMBERS.

445. To the old-time seaman, the middle watch at night wasn't called graveyard but rather "gravy-eye" because the eyes at that time seemed to feel sticky from lack of sleep. What are the hours of this watch?

446. Today, what is the last floating link with the entire White Star fleet?

447. In a sea chantey does the phrase "Blow the man down" refer to wind?

448. What were the colors used on the funnels of the Italian Line?

445.   MIDNIGHT TO 4:00 A.M.

446.   *NOMADIC,* A 220-FOOT PASSENGER TENDER, BUILT IN
        1911 AT HARLAND & WOLFF TO SERVICE THE NEW GIANTS
        OLYMPIC AND *TITANIC,* IS TODAY MOORED ALONG THE
        SEINE IN PARIS.

447.   BLOW IN THIS SENSE MEANS A BLOW WITH A FIST.

448.   RED, WHITE AND GREEN.

449. To what group of islands does Tahiti belong?

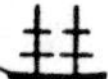

450. What were the highly decorated structures built at the bows and sterns of galleons called?

451. Could "Don't send a boy to do a man's job" possibly have a nautical background? If so, how?

452. Who wrote *The Sea Devil*, concerning Count Felix Von Luckner, who sank fourteen ships?

453. Which ship had more bidets: *Queen Mary* or *Andrea Doria?*

449.　　SOCIETY ISLANDS.

450.　　CASTLES, THE NAMES FORECASTLE AND AFTERCASTLE OUTLIVED THEIR ORIGINAL APPLICATION.

451.　　THIS IS ACTUALLY AN OLD NAUTICAL SAYING, AS IN SAILING DAYS IT TOOK STRONG MEN TO HANDLE THE LARGE CANVAS SAILS.

452.　　LOWELL THOMAS.

453.　　*ANDREA DORIA* HAD BIDETS IN ALL FIRST CLASS CABINS. *QUEEN MARY* HAD THEM ONLY IN HER SUITES.

454. What was the first ship (liner) to be launched by a reigning monarch?

455. On a small vessel would the word *caboose* be synonymous with the word *galley?*

456. What was the first ship to offer first class suites with their own private terraces?

457. Were dungarees first worn on shore or on ships?

458. What was England's largest port until 1922?

454.   THE *SOUTHERN CROSS* WAS CHRISTENED BY QUEEN ELIZABETH II IN 1954.

455.   YES — ON A SMALL BOAT THE CABOOSE IS A CABIN OR DECKHOUSE.

456.   THE *NORMANDIE,* 1935.

457.   THE WORD DUNGAREES WAS FIRST APPLIED TO CLOTHES WORN BY SAILORS — IT IS OF HINDUSTANI ORIGIN.

458.   LIVERPOOL.

459. What was the name of the research ship from Woods Hole Oceanographic Institute in Massachusetts that was involved in finding the *Titanic?*

460. What is another word that means a school of whales?

461. What ships were the first to have kosher kitchens?

462. A land mile is greater than a sea mile—true or false?

463. Where is the transom located on a boat?

459.　　THE *KNORR.*

460.　　POD.

461.　　ALBERT BALLIN'S "IMPERATOR" CLASS.

462.　　FALSE.　A SEA MILE IS GREATER.

463.　　THE STERN.

464.   What 1,000-foot White Star liner was abandoned shortly after her keel was laid?

465.   What would a British seaman mean if he said at the scene of a wreck, "I've found another Hugh Williams"?

466.   What was the name of the sister ship of the *Michelangelo?*

467.   Are ships always referred to as "she"?

468.   What is the full name of the type of davit used on the *Queen Mary?*

464. THE *OCEANIC,* TO BE 60,000 TONS, WAS LAID DOWN AT HARLAND & WOLFF IN 1928, TWO AND A HALF YEARS AHEAD OF THE *QUEEN MARY.* SHE WOULD HAVE BEEN THE FIRST 1,000-FOOT SHIP.

465. HE WOULD MEAN THAT HE HAD FOUND THE SOLE SUR-VIVOR. ACCORDING TO RECORDS, OVER THIRTY SUR-VIVORS (IN A 200-YEAR PERIOD) HAVE BEEN NAMED HUGH WILLIAMS.

466. THE *RAFFAELLO.*

467. YES, BUT THERE WAS A TYPE OF SHIP CALLED A *MAN-OF-WAR.* NEVERTHELESS, IN ALL ROMANCE LANGUAGES "SHIP" IS OF THE FEMALE GENDER.

468. THE TAYLOR GRAVITY DAVIT.

469. Name the novel feature of the ballroom on the *Bremen* (1929).

470. In the year 1940, what ship had the greatest variety of woods used in her interior decoration?

471. Who presided over the American inquiry into the loss of the *Titanic?*

472. What river is the only one in North America that flows *up* (from Cape Canaveral to Jacksonville, Florida)?

473. What liner is the Russian immigrant Vladimir Yourkevitch chiefly responsible for designing?

469.   IT HAD A FOUNTAIN THAT SPRAYED PERFUMED WATER.

470.   THE *QUEEN ELIZABETH.*

471.   SENATOR WILLIAM ALDEN SMITH.

472.   ST. JOHN'S RIVER.

473.   THE GREAT FRENCH LINER *NORMANDIE.*

474. What waterway in Cornwall, England is the title of a book by Daphne du Maurier?

475. What was the last four-funneled liner in service?

476. Who was the first United States President to sail his own vessel to a foreign port?

477. What kind of sea-going creature is a "thresher"?

478. What is the name of the protective rail running around the edge of most table tops and bureaus on board ship?

474.   FRENCHMAN'S CREEK. IT IS PRESENTLY PRESERVED BY THE NATIONAL TRUST. A LEAFY TUNNEL IS SHELTERED BY TREES; A GREAT PLACE FOR SMALL-CRAFT SAILORS AND ROMANTICS.

475.   THE *AQUITANIA*, 1914 - 1950.

476.   FRANKLIN D. ROOSEVELT TOOK HIS SCHOONER TO CAMPOBELLO, CANADA.

477.   A SHARK WITH A GREATLY ELONGATED CURVED UPPER LOBE OF ITS TAIL. IT THRESHES ITS TAIL AROUND IN THE WATER TO ROUND UP FISH TO EAT.

478.   FIDDLE-BOARDS.

479. Would you say a sailor on a ship "stands watch" or "keeps watch"?

480. In the 1930's, what were weekend cruises often called?

481. What do the initials "R.M.S." stand for before a ship's name?

482. Does "Dutch courage" refer to brass knuckles or a shot of liquor?

483. *Savarona* cost $4,000,000. What was her distinction?

479.   STANDS WATCH. "STAND BY" IS PROBABLY ALSO DERIVED
        FROM THE PRACTICE OF ONE NAVAL SHIP REMAINING
        CLOSE TO ANOTHER VESSEL TO GIVE ASSISTANCE IF
        NEEDED.

480.   "BOOZE CRUISES."

481.   ROYAL MAIL SHIP (OR STEAMER).

482.   LIQUOR WHICH THE DUTCH NAVY SUPPOSEDLY SERVED
        THEIR SAILORS BEFORE BATTLE.

483.   THE LARGEST PRIVATE SAILING YACHT EVER BUILT. Mrs.
        Emily Roebling Cadwalader had it constructed in Hamburg,
        Germany, in 1931. It was 407 feet, 10 inches overall and was sold
        to the Turkish government in 1938.

484. What ship carried a large metal sculpture of an eagle at the bow?

485. East Chop and Gay Head lighthouses are located on what island?

486. What flag is flown by most ocean-going vessels when they are about to leave port?

487. Under present maritime law, is it allowable to fly more than one club pennant at a time, even though you may be a member of several clubs?

484.   THE *IMPERATOR*.

485.   MARTHA'S VINEYARD.

486.   THE "P" SIGNAL FLAG, USUALLY CALLED THE "BLUE PETER."

487.   IT'S ALLOWABLE BUT NOT REGARDED AS GOOD FORM.

488. In the old days the position of stewardess was much sought after on the great transatlantic liners. How was one most likely given this job?

489. What ship was used in the laying of the first Atlantic cable in 1865?

490. A restaurant in New York called One Fifth Avenue has portholes and light fixtures salvaged from what ocean liner?

491. Where is the only *Titanic* monument in the world that actually shows the ship dramatically at a steep angle just before sinking into the ocean?

488.   THESE POSITIONS WERE MOSTLY GIVEN TO THE RELATIVES OF MEN WHO HAD DIED WHILE IN THAT COMPANY'S SERVICE.

489.   THE *GREAT EASTERN.*

490.   THE S.S. *CARONIA.*

491.   SAINT JOHN'S STAINED GLASS WINDOW IN ST. JOHN'S CHURCH IN NEW YORK. The stained glass monument is dedicated to John Jacob Astor and other victims of the *Titanic* disaster. This scene forms a small part of Ernest Lakeman's (1941) enormous cathedral window.

492. Instead of the riveting of ships, what has commonly been done since World War II?

493. What U.S. ship at the present time has the largest guns?

494. What rank is the highest officer in the British navy?

495. What is another expression for a blanket aboard ship?

496. What does it mean to "Dress Ship"?

492.   WELDING.

493.   THE U.S.S. *IOWA*.

494.   ADMIRAL OF THE FLEET.

495.   A "STEAMER RUG."

496.   TO HOIST FLAGS ON SPECIAL OCCASIONS. WHEN FLAGS
        ARE FLOWN FROM THE MAST TOPS, THE SHIP IS SAID TO
        BE "DRESSED."

497. Chamber pots were used on the *Lusitania, Mauretania,* and even *Queen Mary.* True or false?

498. What does the prefix "H.M.S." stand for before a ship's name?

499. On the eve of World War I, whose likeness (picture) appeared in all German ships?

500. In Sausalito, California, a persistent underwater hum annoyed residents of houseboats for more than ten years. The noise was loud enough to wake people and drown out conversation. What was the source?

501. What U.S. battleship was known affectionately as *"Big Mamie"?*

497.   TRUE. ALL CLASSES ON THE *LUSITANIA* AND THE *MAURE-TANIA* HAD CHAMBER POTS, AS DID THIRD CLASS ON THE *QUEEN MARY.*

498.   HIS OR HER MAJESTY'S SHIP. THESE INITIALS WERE FIRST USED IN 1789 IN REFERENCE TO H.M.S. *PHOENIX.*

499.   KAISER WILHELM II.

500.   SINGING TOADFISH (MALE) LOOKING FOR FEMALE COMPANY.

501.   U.S.S. *MASSACHUSETTS.*

502. The most effective device yet found for protecting swimmers in shark-infested areas was instigated by the Australians. What is it called?

503. What British king was known as "The Sailor King"?

504. What explorer who discovered Delaware Bay had a ship named *Half Moon?*

505. Is the statement that the boat which has the right of way is known as the privileged vessel true or false?

506. What kind of fishery in California was immortalized by John Steinbeck's novel *Cannery Row?*

502. "MESHING" — OR PUTTING OUT NETS. The nets were first tried in Sydney in 1937, and in the first year 1,500 sharks were captured. The loosely hanging nets set in place overnight entangle sharks, which are then killed.

503. KING WILLIAM IV.

504. HENRY HUDSON.

505. THE STATEMENT IS TRUE.

506. A SARDINE CANNERY.

507. In the days of square riggers, what color band was painted around the entire hull when a captain or officer was lost during a voyage?

508. What lighthouse was commissioned by George Washington?

509. What was the nickname given to the long, plain, black knickers (or underwear) issued to the WRENS (Women's Royal Navy Service) in World War II?

510. How did the term *head* happen to be used to refer to a ship's toilet?

507. A BLUE BAND. ALSO, BLUE FLAGS WERE FLOWN. PERHAPS THAT'S WHERE "FEELING BLUE" CAME FROM.

508. MONTAUK POINT LIGHT. It was built on Washington's orders 400 feet from the sea so that it might survive 200 years. Erosion has taken its toll and experts predict that less than 50 feet will remain between the sea and the lighthouse at the 200 year mark. Giorgina and Don Reid (along with the Montauk Point Erosion Control Project, Inc.) have been instrumental in controlling soil erosion.

509. "PASSION KILLERS."

510. BECAUSE THIS FACILITY WAS LOCATED AT THE HEAD (OR BOW) OF A SHIP IN THE OLD DAYS. SAILORS USED TO HANG ON FOR DEAR LIFE WHILE BALANCING ON THE JIB BOOM.

511. In the early 20th century, what did Queenstown, Plymouth, Cherbourg and Gibraltar have in common, with reference to passengers embarking and disembarking transatlantic ships?

512. What ship introduced plastic composition bathroom door knobs that were "warm to the touch"?

513. What ship disaster prompted the formation of the International Ice Patrol?

514. What was the name of the affliction which passengers suffered by trying to open their own portholes?

511.   THEY ALL NEEDED SMALL BOATS (*TENDERS*) FOR PAS-
        SENGERS TO GET TO OR FROM LAND, AS NONE OF THESE
        CITIES HAD DOCKING FACILITIES DEEP ENOUGH TO
        ACCOMMODATE THE LARGE TRANSATLANTIC SHIPS.

512.   THE *QUEEN MARY.* PLASTIC WAS USED INSTEAD OF METAL
        FOR PASSENGER COMFORT WHENEVER POSSIBLE, ON
        HANDLES, DOOR KNOBS, RAILINGS AND SUCH.

513.   THE *TITANIC* DISASTER.

514.   PORTHOLE THUMB.

515. In the 1920's, Cunard provided a weekly New York to Southampton sailing schedule, using what three ships?

516. What is the name of a particular type of cloth (thin and light, but strong) that is woven to serve well for signal flags on ships?

517. Is there any fixed interval at which a larger than average wave can be predicted—such as the third, ninth or tenth wave?

518. What is the derivation of the word life-*buoy*?

519. What is unusual about the beach at Harbour Island, near Eleuthera, in the Bahamas?

515. THE *MAURETANIA, AQUITANIA* AND *BERENGARIA.*

516. BUNTING.

517. NO, THERE IS NO FIXED INTERVAL.

518. MERELY DROPPING THE LAST THREE LETTERS OF THE WORD "BUOYANT" WHICH MEANS FLOATING.

519. IT IS PALE PINK DUE TO PULVERIZED CORAL — IT IS ALSO VERY SOFT.

520. What is a young seal called?

521. Which of the following forms of address would be
      appropriately applied to a captain of a ship?
      1. Captain Smith.
      2. Captain Bill.
      3. Skipper.

522. What was the name of the ship that, during the
      Second World War, struck a German mine while
      carrying £2,500,000 worth of gold bullion?

523. What passenger ship (in a disaster in May of 1914)
      sank more quickly than any other ship on record?

520.   A PUP.

521.   #1. OR #2.   BUT NEVER SKIPPER. ONLY MASTERS OF BARGES OR HARBOR CRAFT MIGHT BE CALLED SKIPPER.

522.   THE *NIAGARA*. THE BULLION WAS RECOVERED.

523.   THE *EMPRESS OF IRELAND*, ON THE NIGHT OF MAY 28, 1914, COLLIDED WITH A NORWEGIAN FREIGHTER AND SANK IN LESS THAN *FIFTEEN* MINUTES.

524. Who made the fastest voyage around the world in a sailing vessel which was fifty-four feet overall and thirty-nine and a half feet on the waterline?

525. In 1856 Gail Borden invented something that was to prove a boon to voyagers on the sea and elsewhere. What was this?

526. What was the fastest liner ever to sail the seas?

527. The first of a new breed of American battleships (commissioned in 1941) was nicknamed "The Showboat." What was the actual name of this ship that participated in many battles in the Pacific during World War II?

524.   SIR FRANCIS CHICHESTER IN *GIPSY MOTH IV.*

525.   CANNED OR CONDENSED MILK WAS ORIGINALLY INVENTED
        SO THAT COWS WOULD NOT HAVE TO BE CARRIED ABOARD
        SHIPS TO SUPPLY MILK FOR BABIES.

526.   THE *UNITED STATES,* WHICH CAPTURED THE RECORD IN
        1952 BY A WIDE MARGIN AND WAS CAPABLE OF OVER
        38 KNOTS.

527.   U.S.S. *NORTH CAROLINA.*

528. How is the expression "The Brass Monkey" connected with the Cunard Steamship Line?

529. In 1985 the Home Lines launched a 35,000-ton
passenger liner. What was her name?

530. A *kelpie* is:
    1. A Scottish spirit.
    2. A fish of the cod variety.
    3. The ashes of seaweed used as a source of
       iodine.

531. What town in New England has the largest ship
model (nearly 60 feet in length) in the world, the
bark *Lagoda,* currently on display in the Whaling
Museum?

528. IT IS THE NICKNAME FOR THE HANDSOME GOLDEN LION ON THE CUNARD HOUSE-FLAG.

529. THE *HOMERIC*.

530. #1. A SCOTTISH SPIRIT.

531. NEW BEDFORD, MASSACHUSETTS.

532. What was the first ship to have a complete restaurant opened separately from the dining saloons?

533. At the present time "high seas" begin three miles off the United States shore—true or false?

534. The ship *Queen Elizabeth 2* is named after the reigning monarch of Britain—true or false?

535. Who was the first person to order the use of hammocks, in which sailors could sleep?

536. After the Cunard Line acquired the *Imperator* (sister to the *Bismarck*), what did they name her?

532.   THE *AMERIKA* (IN 1908) HAD THE RITZ-CARLTON.

533.   FALSE. At last research (in a dictionary of nautical terms) high seas begin anywhere from 12 to 100 miles offshore. Interest in oil and fishing rights has changed the definition of high seas. In days gone by, high seas was designated at three miles because that was supposedly the utmost range of a cannon. The limit of "high seas" or "international waters" may be greater by now.

534.   FALSE. Often mis-labelled *Queen Elizabeth II* (the second), QE2 (two) is named, in fact, after the great ship of the same name which preceded her.

535.   COLUMBUS. HE DISCOVERED THEIR PRACTICAL USE FROM THE NATIVES IN THE WEST INDIES.

536.   THE *BERENGARIA.*

537. A rectangular blue flag with 50 white stars is called a ___________ ___________ .

538. What is pharology?

539. In the world of old salts what do the words "bible leaves," "blanket pieces," and "horse pieces" refer to?

540. Legend has it that *Queen Mary* was not the originally planned name for hull 534 at John Brown's shipyard prior to the Cunard-White Star merger. What *was* her name to be?

541. What liner, much to the dismay of its owners, was infested with fleas in the 1930's?

537.   UNION JACK.

538.   THE SCIENCE OF LIGHTHOUSE ENGINEERING.

539.   WHALES. THESE TERMS REFER TO THE OPERATION OF PEELING THE BLUBBER OFF THE WHALE BEFORE GETTING IT READY TO BE REDUCED TO OIL BY BOILING IN LARGE POTS.

540.   *VICTORIA*, IN KEEPING WITH CUNARD'S TRADITION OF NAMING ALL ITS SHIPS WITH AN "IA" ENDING.

541.   *REX.*

542. In early seafaring times, when they said of a man "he knows the ropes," did that mean he was an expert sailor?

543. The four funnels of the *Lusitania* were spaced evenly. True or false?

544. What is a baby shark called (besides dangerous)?

545. Who wrote *Stalking the Blue-Eyed Scallop?*

546. Is Cape Horn so named because it is shaped like a horn?

542.   NO, NOT NECESSARILY. THIS PHRASE WAS WRITTEN ON HIS DISCHARGE, MEANING THAT HE WAS A NOVICE, THAT ALL HE KNEW WAS THE NAMES AND USES OF ROPES.

543.   FALSE. THERE WAS A VARIANCE OF AS MUCH AS 3 FEET, THE WIDEST SPACE BEING IN THE CENTER.

544.   A CUB.

545.   EUELL GIBBONS.

546.   NO. CAPTAIN SCHOUTEN, THE DUTCH NAVIGATOR WHO FOUNDED IT IN 1616, NAMED IT AFTER HOORN, HIS BIRTH-PLACE IN NORTHERN HOLLAND.

547. The FCC booklet "How To Use Your VHF Marine Radio" cautions mariners not to use Channel 88A. Why?

548. "In the dog house" is an old seafaring term dating back to the 1800's. In our usage it means being somewhere we don't want to be, in someone's disfavor or in a bad spot. In early days the term came from:
1. Pirates.
2. The slave trade.
3. Neither of the above.

549. Is it true or false that the Navy almost always named battleships for states and cruisers after cities?

550. What two locations in Maine originally had "twin lights," two lighthouses in close proximity to each other?

547.   IT IS RESERVED EXCLUSIVELY FOR COMMERCIAL BOAT OWNERS (AT LEAST ON THE WEST COAST.)

548.   #2.   In days gone by slaves were squeezed into every conceivable niche aboard a ship — even in the officers' quarters. Sometimes the officers had to sleep on the poop deck in a very small cubicle about six or seven feet long. The uncomfortable enclosures were nicknamed "dog-houses."

549.   TRUE. THE U.S. NAVY DID BREAK WITH TRADITION IN NAMING A SHIP FOR A LIVING PERSON BY NAMING A SHIP AFTER ADMIRAL HYMAN G. RICKOVER.

550.   CAPE ELIZABETH AND MATINICUS ROCK. One of the lighthouses on Cape Elizabeth (including the keepers' dwelling) was recently sold to an individual for private use. The asking price was over $300,000.

551. In children's literature did "Li'l Red" refer to:
1. A tugboat.
2. A lighthouse.
3. A dog that loved the sea.

552. What is an old boat that has seen better days called? It is a term synonymous with the name for a lady of ill repute.

553. What is the mythical heaven of sailors called?

554. At least 7,000 military personnel and civilians in flight from an avenging Red army perished when a Russian submarine torpedoed this ship in the Baltic Sea in 1945. Name the ship.

551.   IT REFERS TO *THE LITTLE RED LIGHTHOUSE AND THE GREAT GRAY BRIDGE* BY HILDEGARDE SWIFT AND LYND WARD ABOUT THE LIGHT UNDER THE GEORGE WASHINGTON BRIDGE IN MANHATTAN.

552.   A "HOOKER" FROM THE DUTCH WORD *HOEKER* MEANING AN OLD, AWKWARD FISHING BOAT.

553.   FIDDLER'S GREEN.

554.   *WILHELM GUSTLOFF.* THE TRAGEDY IS THE WORST LOSS OF LIFE EVER IN THE ANNALS OF MARITIME HISTORY, NEARLY FIVE TIMES THE NUMBER LOST IN THE *TITANIC* DISASTER.

555. What shipyard built nearly all the White Star vessels?

556. Are there in actuality more than seven seas in the world?

557. During the days of massive U.S.-bound immigration, steerage passengers often chose ships with the most funnels. Accordingly, shipowners were sometimes known to rig two or three extra "funnels" of canvas for use in European ports. True or false?

558. In the Navy what nickname is a ship's cook often given?

555.   HARLAND & WOLFF, LTD., BELFAST, IRELAND.

556.   YES, THERE ARE MORE LIKE 75 SEAS.

557.   TRUE, ACCORDING TO *FORTUNE* MAGAZINE, JUNE, 1936.

558.   "DOC."

559. In 1984 a British sailing barque sank in a fierce squall off Bermuda while participating in the Tall Ships Race from Bermuda to Halifax. Nine of the 28 persons on board were rescued. What was the name of this ship?

560. In which month does the Regatta at Henley-on-Thames at Oxfordshire, England begin every year?

561. In what country was the founder of the American Navy, John Paul Jones, born?

562. The pirate Bartholomew Roberts (1682-1722) was credited with having taken over 400 ships. Which, if any, of the following statements about Roberts are false?
1. He was a teetotaler.
2. He allowed no women on his ship.
3. He allowed no gambling on his ship.

559.   THE *MARQUES.*

560.   AT THE BEGINNING OF JULY FOR FOUR DAYS.

561.   SCOTLAND.

562.   NONE OF THE STATEMENTS ARE FALSE. BARTHOLOMEW
        ROBERTS (ONE OF THE WORLD'S GREAT PIRATES) WAS
        NOTED FOR HIS REMARKABLE DISCIPLINE.

563. Who wrote *The Sea Around Us?*

564. Who was the first Captain of the QE2?

565. Who is considered the "father of the nuclear sub-marine"?

566. What are the lines, ropes or tackles used to hoist or lower sails called?

567. What does "Kilroy was here" have to do with nautical matters?

563.   RACHEL CARSON.

564.   WILLIAM E. WARWICK.

565.   ADMIRAL HYMAN GEORGE RICKOVER, WHO SAW TO THE BUILDING OF THE FIRST NUCLEAR SUB, *NAUTILUS*, LAUNCHED IN 1952.

566.   HALYARDS.

567.   JAMES J. KILROY (who was an inspector in a Quincy, Massachusetts shipyard) chalked the words "KILROY WAS HERE" on ships and crates of equipment to indicate they had been inspected. He died in Boston in 1962.

568. Name the three means of propulsion available to the *Great Eastern* (1857).

569. Name the place that the following words describe:
1. The largest island in the Baltic—belonging to Sweden.
2. Has more than 700 Bronze Age ship-form stone graves.
3. Sweden's playground (with fine sand beaches) for Stockholm's rich set.

570. What is another name for a coal ship?

571. What does the "U" stand for in U-boat?

568.   PADDLE WHEELS, SCREW PROPELLER AND SAILS.

569.   GOTLAND.

570.   A "COLLIER."

571.   "UNTERSEE," THE GERMAN WORD FOR "UNDERSEA," OR "SUBMARINE."

*

572. In the British navy, when someone says that a person is an "O.D.," what does he mean?
   1. He is an officer and has an "overdose" of conceit.
   2. He is an ordinary seaman.
   3. He is a chaplain in the Anglican Church and a member of the Order of Divinity.

573. The porpoise is the fastest swimming sea animal. True or false?

574. What superstition do sailors have concerning hatch covers?

575. Was it from Harwich or Plymouth, England that the original *Mayflower* set sail for America?

572.   #2.   HE IS AN ORDINARY SEAMAN. TAKEN FROM THE FIRST AND THIRD LETTERS OF THE WORD "ORDINARY."

573.   FALSE.   MARLIN, BONITO, ALBACORE, SAILFISH AND SWORDFISH HAVE BEEN KNOWN TO SWIM 60 MILES PER HOUR.

574.   HATCH COVERS LEFT UPSIDE DOWN ON DECK ARE BAD LUCK BECAUSE IN THE OLD DAYS IT WAS THOUGHT THAT SUCH CARELESSNESS WOULD GIVE EVIL SPIRITS ACCESS TO THE CARGO AND, CONSEQUENTLY, POWER TO BEWITCH.

575.   CONTRARY TO POPULAR BELIEF, IT WAS FROM HARWICH.

576. All that remains of the original *Queen Elizabeth* is its huge anchor, which stands 20 feet tall and 15 feet across, and weighs 22 tons. Where is it now located?
1. Washington, D.C.
2. Torrance, California.
3. Southampton, England.

577. In *Ring of Bright Water,* did the author write about an otter, porpoise or a shark?

578. Why does the pulpit at the Seaman's Bethel chapel in New Bedford, Massachusetts remind one of the pulpit described in the book *Moby Dick?*

579. What famous English hero said, "At sea nothing is impossible and nothing improbable"?

576. #2. The cast iron anchor has found a permanent home at the American Asian Bank on Carson Street in Torrance, California. The *Queen Elizabeth* was renamed *Seawise University*, caught fire, and sank in Hong Kong Harbor in 1971.

577. *RING OF BRIGHT WATER* BY GAVIN MAXWELL IS ABOUT A PET OTTER.

578. BECAUSE THE PULPIT AT THE SEAMAN'S BETHEL AT 15 JOHNNY CAKE HILL IS SHAPED LIKE THE BOW OF A SHIP JUST AS IN *MOBY DICK*.

579. LORD NELSON.

580. Who (of the following) owns Jekyll Island off the coast of Georgia?
    1. Vanderbilts.
    2. Rockefellers.
    3. The state of Georgia.

581. In what city (in the United States) is the Navy's largest installation as to ships and manpower?

582. The last *male* stowaway on the *Queen Mary* was 31-year-old Tom Barry, who was caught by Robin Davies, now working on the *QE2*. In what port was Barry caught?

583. What was the name of the cruise ship which was hijacked in October of 1985?

580.   #3.   JEKYLL ISLAND, ONCE A RETREAT FOR MILLIONAIRES, IS NOW STATE-OWNED BY GEORGIA.

581.   SAN DIEGO, CALIFORNIA.

582.   SOUTHAMPTON.

583.   *ACHILLE LAURO* (ITALIAN REGISTRY).

584. The motto of the Coast Guard is *"Semper Paratus."* What is the English translation?

585. In the seaside town of Zennor in England there is a church that houses a "Mermaid Chair." The mermaid is said to have lured chorister Matthew Trevella down to the sea beneath the cliffs of Zennor Head. The pair was never seen again. In the "Mermaid Chair," what does the mermaid have in each hand? Hint: most mermaids are never without these items.

586. Who said, "We are dressed in our best and prepared to go down like gentlemen" when confronted with a maritime disaster?

587. In days gone by, did the regular sailors or the officers live in the forward part of a sailing ship?

584.   "ALWAYS READY."

585.   THE MERMAID HAS A COMB IN ONE HAND AND A MIRROR IN THE OTHER.

586.   BENJAMIN GUGGENHEIM, WHEN HE HEARD THE *TITANIC* WAS GOING TO SINK.

587.   THE CREW LIVED IN THE FORWARD LIVING QUARTERS: "BEFORE THE MAST."

588. What ever happened to Captain Joshua Slocum (who was one of the greatest mariners of all time) in 1909?

589. In naval terminology what does the term "Dead Horse" mean?

590. Why are sailor's trousers shaped in a bell-bottom design?

591. The last lighthouse operated in the United States, before one reaches the Mexican-U.S. border, is Brazos Santiago Lighthouse on Padre Island. Near what town in Texas is this lighthouse located.

592. How did the name "quarterdeck" come to apply to ships?

588.   HE SAILED OVER THE HORIZON IN HIS BOAT *SPRAY* AND WAS NEVER SEEN AGAIN.

589.   ADVANCED PAY THAT MUST BE WORKED OFF. SOMETIMES A MOCK HORSE (MADE OF STRAW) WAS BURNED ABOARD SHIP AS A SYMBOL OF THE DEBT BEING WORKED OFF.

590.   BECAUSE THEY ARE EASIER TO ROLL UP WHEN A SAILOR IS SWABBING THE DECK.

591.   BROWNSVILLE, TEXAS. Although this is a relatively unknown light, Texans continue to do things in a unique way. Dick Daugird built a lighthouse miles from the sea (between Houston and Galveston). It fulfills his fantasy of living in a lighthouse and also houses his insurance office.

592.   DECKS IN THE GOOD (?) OLD DAYS WERE DIVIDED INTO TIERS: FOR EXAMPLE, THE *HALF DECK* AND THE *QUARTERDECK* THUS BEING HALF OF THAT.

593. What is the term for the sailing of a newly-commissioned vessel with the purpose of training the crew and testing the machinery?
    1. A maiden voyage.
    2. A "Bristol-shape" cruise.
    3. A shakedown cruise.

594. According to the English and American measurements, how many nautical miles comprise a league?

595. Katherine Anne Porter wrote a book called *Ship of Fools*, and previously in 1494 Sebastian Brandt wrote *Narrenschiff* which means the same thing in German. In history were there ever any actual ships referred to as *Narrenschiffs?*

596. In navy lingo "Pride of the Morning" is:
    1. The flag raising ceremony.
    2. A morning mist often seen before a fine day.
    3. The name of a famous racing-cutter.
    4. A nip of booze before noon.

593.   #3.   A SHAKEDOWN CRUISE.

594.   THREE NAUTICAL MILES.

595.   YES, in fifteenth century Germany the insane were picked up off the streets and forced to ride up and down the Rhine imprisoned on boats until they reached their final destination which was, of course, death.

596.   A MORNING MIST.

597. Aboard Nelson's *Victory* was a type of ammunition called *hot shot.* What was this?

598. Were birds actually ever carried in the "crow's nest" of a ship?

599. What famous American poet was a frequent visitor to Donald McKay's shipbuilding yard (in the 1850's) and was present at the construction of the *Flying Cloud,* clipper ship? Hint: This poet also wrote "Paul Revere's Ride."

600. "They that go down to the sea in ships, That do business in great waters ..."—from what book are these two lines?

597.   *HOT SHOT* WERE ORDINARY CANNON BALLS HEATED WHITE-HOT BEFORE BEING SHOT OUT OF THE CANNONS AT THE ENEMY SHIPS TO SET THEM AFIRE.

598.   YES, THE NORSEMEN CARRIED RAVENS AT THE TOP OF THEIR MASTHEADS AND WHEN THEY LOST SIGHT OF LAND, THEY WOULD RELEASE ONE OF THE BIRDS AND ITS FLIGHT TO SHORE WOULD GUIDE THEM IN THEIR EFFORTS TO LOCATE LAND ONCE MORE.

599.   HENRY WADSWORTH LONGFELLOW.

600.   THE BIBLE. PSALM 107:23-24. IT CONTINUES: "THESE SEE THE WORKS OF THE LORD, AND HIS WONDERS IN THE DEEP."

Stern view of *Mauretania*
(Ken Marschall collection).

THE END.

About the Author

Rustie Brown is an award-winning newspaper writer and columnist. In 1972, while working for the *Palos Verdes/Lomita News*, she won the coveted Arnold McCartney Memorial Award for "Reporter of the Year" who had done the most to further the ideals of the journalistic profession. In 1976 she was presented a Merit Award from the Pacific Coast Press Club for "Best Feature Story" in a non-daily newspaper. In 1978 she earned the "Award of Excellence" from the California Press Women (an affiliate of the National Federation of Press Women) for "Best Critic's Review." She is an active member of the Titanic Historical Society.

She has done reviews and articles for such diverse publications as *Fate, Dance, Skating, American West, South Bay* magazine, *Bestways* and the *Los Angeles Times*. She is past President of the Southwest Manuscripters (the second female ever to hold that office in the club's thirty-year existence).

Rustie Brown was born in Chicago. She attended Wayland Academy, Towne School, Goodman Theatre and the University of Arizona. She is married and has two children. She currently resides in Palos Verdes Shores, California. Her previous nonfiction book *The Titanic, the Psychic and the Sea* is now in its third printing. Rustie Brown's latest manuscript deals with lighthouse lore.

ORDER FORM

Please send _______________ copy (copies) of The Mariner's Trivia Book at $9.95 each (California residents add $.60 sales tax) plus $1.50 postage and handling charges to:

Name ____

Address ____

City _________________________ State__________ Zip ___________

Send check or money order to:
BLUE HARBOR PRESS, P.O. BOX 1028, LOMITA, CA. 90717